Grace Under FIRE

The Journey Never Ends

Dr. Charlotte Russell Johnson

Author of

A Journey to Hell and Back

Grace

It's grace that's so amazing…
It's grace that keeps me praising…
It's grace that stops my misbehaving…
It's Your grace that keeps saving…

Without Your grace, where would I be?
Without Your grace, would Your face I ever see?
Without Your grace would I ever be free?
Without Your grace could You ever love me?

Grace stay close to me…
Grace guides me safely to Thee…
Grace let me hide my sins in Thee…
Grace, Grace, Grace keeps protecting me…

Grace destroys all my fears…
Grace dries all my tears…
Grace covers the pain in my ears…
Grace makes my path so clear…

4

Grace holds me up under fire...
Grace controls all I desire...
Grace, Grace continues to inspire...
It was Grace that lifted me up out of the mire...
By Your Grace even if I fall, I won't retire...

Grace, Grace, God's Great Grace
Help me to finish this race!

Dedication

To Hattie and Ruben Benny Owens for the seeds that you sewed into my life. Also to my very very special niece Darlene, no book would be complete without you.

It is also dedicated to those who have discovered the secrets of longevity in marriage.

In Memory
Of
"Shelena"

May 27, 1973 - July 24, 2004

My heart is still healing from the pain of your loss.

Table of Contents

Preface

*I sinned, but it was not worth it. God rescued
me from the grave, and now my life is filled
with light.* **Job 33:27 NLT**

My first book, *A Journey to Hell and Back* is an
autobiographical account of my life. It details major
events in my life, which almost destroyed me.
However, these events served to make me a stronger
person and more grateful for the loving grace of God.

My second book, *Daddy's Hugs* exhorts the role
of fathers in the lives of children. The book's major
hypothesis is that the role of fathers is the fundamental
element in promoting healthy child development and
self-esteem. The book praises and provides examples of
fathers who take a diligent role in parenting.

My third book *A Journey to Hell and Back: The
Flip Side* tells both sides of the journey. *The Flip Side*
is my husband's version of the events in our lives. We
share our separate struggles, which became a common
struggle. Our lives can only be described as trips to the
very pits of hell. However, beneath it all is a
remarkable testimony of the love and grace of God.

Grace Under Fire is written only after heartfelt
consideration. In my previous books, I deliberately
avoided issues that would be viewed as unfavorable or
controversial to the body of Christ. The church has
been labeled as being full of hypocrites. There may be a
measure of truth in this statement; hypocrites are
everywhere.

Out of necessity, I will discuss some issues that
may be sensitive or disturbing to some. There are some
things that should not be named among the body of

Christ. Those who engage in these acts are often mistakenly identified as Christians. Church membership does not denote salvation or Christianity. Many of the events in this book were done openly and notoriously and then reported to be sanctioned by God. In reading this book, please know that my intentions are not to embarrass anyone. Nevertheless, I intend to expose these deeds of darkness for what they are, an abomination to the body of Christ.

My prayer remains that the lives of those who read these books will be enriched by something written in these books.

All scripture references are from the King James Bible unless otherwise noted.

Ephesians 5:3-17

But fornication, and all uncleanness, or covetousness, let it not be once named among you, as becometh saints; Neither filthiness, nor foolish talking, nor jesting, which are not convenient: but rather giving of thanks. For this ye know, that no whoremonger, nor unclean person, nor covetous man, who is an idolater, hath any inheritance in the kingdom of Christ and of God. Let no man deceive you with vain words: for because of these things cometh the wrath of God upon the children of disobedience. Be not ye therefore partakers with them. For ye were sometimes darkness, but now are ye light in the Lord: walk as children of light: (For the fruit of the Spirit is in all goodness and righteousness and truth;) Proving what is acceptable unto the Lord. And have no fellowship with the unfruitful works of darkness, but rather reprove them. For it is a shame even to speak of those things which are done of them in secret. But all things that are reproved are made manifest by the light: for whatsoever doth make manifest is light. Wherefore He saith, Awake thou that sleepest, and arise from the dead, and Christ shall give thee light. See then that ye walk circumspectly, not as fools, but as wise, Redeeming the time, because the days are evil. Wherefore be ye not unwise, but understanding what the will of the Lord is.

Introduction by Earline Hall

In *Grace Under Fire: The Journey Never Ends,* author Charlotte Russell Johnson coins the fourth installment in her series of motivational text. Ms. Johnson continues to share the intimate and personal events in her life to offer encouragement to those suffering. In this text, Ms. Johnson's writing evolves emotionally. The reader is able to view her innermost secrets and emotions. The reader is seduced by the lust of the characters for love and money, while secretly retaining a desire to see their ultimate redemption. These complex characters and their labyrinth of romantic entanglements rival F. Scott Fitzgerald's *The Great Gatsby.*

The author explores the importance of hope, love, and forgiveness in marriage. This book is excellent for anyone who has experienced love, heartache, betrayal, deception, divorce, remarriage, anticipates becoming married, or working with any of these populations.

They say that you should never burn the bridge that has brought you through, but at what point is the bridge a safety hazard? This is the first question Ms. Johnson leaves the reader pondering. If it is true when one door closes another opens, what should you do when the wind continues to open and shut both doors simultaneously? After reading *Grace Under Fire*, these and many other questions will spark spirited debates.

Ms. Johnson is able to hold the reader spellbound and enchanted until the book's surprise ending. Ms. Johnson invites the reader to view her life and experience love, grace, and redemption.

The Alarm Sounds

Surely the Lord GOD will do nothing, but He revealeth His secret unto His servants the prophets.
Amos 3:7

The Bible tells us clearly that a warning always precedes destruction. It always does. I should know; it appears destruction has aimed for my life from the beginning. Maybe, it wasn't destruction. Maybe, my life wasn't the target. It is a certainty that I have fought many battles against destruction. God always warns His people before destruction comes. It's our choice to heed or ignore these warnings.

It can be extremely difficult to be the bearer of news that has a negative content. The message is often rejected or ignored. How much more difficult it is to receive a message that something adverse is about to happen in your life!

In everything you do, stay away from complaining and arguing, so that no one can speak a word of blame against you. You are to live clean, innocent lives as children of God in a dark world full of crooked and perverse people. Let your lives shine brightly before them. Hold tightly to the word of life, so that when Christ returns, I will be proud that I did not lose the race and that my work was not useless. **Philippians 2:14-16 NLT**

Several years ago, my mother told me about a message that she had received from the Lord. She shared this message with me, "There are going to be some hard days ahead. You will have to be rooted and grounded to be able to stand."

The message was not directed specifically to me. This was a global message. Since every word of prophecy spoken from her lips had found fertile ground in the past, I knew these words were true. This conversation occurred shortly before September 11. Immediately, we began to meet people everywhere who were in crisis. Strangers began to share their problems with us.

We are confident that as you share in suffering, you will also share God's comfort.
2 Corinthians 1:7 NLT

Later, she spoke another word, "The whole world is in turmoil."

I didn't feel immune from these prophecies. However, because of the measure of grace God had given me in the past, I was confident that, by His grace, I would survive anything. These prophecies posed no immediate threat to my life. Therefore, I developed a false sense of security. There was turmoil all around me. In spite of this, I was basking in His grace. God was continuing to show me unmerited favor. My life was finally on track. Things were destined to change.

In every battle you will need faith as your shield to stop the fiery arrows aimed at you by Satan. **Ephesians 6:16 NLT**

It began before September 11. God began to push me to write my first book. I was struggling to maintain my life according to the *status quo*. A number of things happened to get me to accept the challenge. This includes being terminated from two jobs without justification for the terminations.

The thief's purpose is to steal and kill and destroy. My purpose is to give life in all its fullness. **John 10:10 NLT**

After I wrote *A Journey to Hell and Back*, there was a period of calm. Actually, things began to go so well that it was often scary. The storm was already on the horizon. I had missed the weather forecast. When things began to go wrong, I viewed them as isolated incidents. The alarm had sounded without me hearing it. This storm was going to ignite a fire.

Be not far from me; for trouble is near; for there is none to help… **Psalm 22:11**

Some things in my life have changed; nevertheless, others things have remained the same. At least, they appear to be the same. So many good things have happened. Yet, at times, it appears so many bad things preceded the good things that happened. God has been true to His Word. The bad things have all worked out for my good.

There is fire and then there is fire. There is grace and then there is grace. If it becomes necessary, there is more grace. For me fire came twice. Both times, by God's grace, my life was spared. There were other times when things in my life became so heated that it felt like fire. Grace came countless times and continues to come.

Ma'Dear

Since I know it is all for Christ's good, I am
quite content with my weaknesses and with
insults, hardships, persecutions, and
calamities. For when I am weak, then I am
strong. **2 Corinthians 12:10 NLT**

My grandmother, Earline Emmaline Nettie Pearl Odessa Owens was a unique and distinct person. She was as special her name. I could never get her to acknowledge this as her full legal name; however, my great grandmother, Mae insisted she had indeed given her daughter, this unique name at her birth. Ma'Dear was named after each of Mae's aunts. Later, Ma'Dear married Theodore Alexander and added another name to the long list.

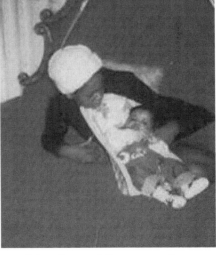

To her friends, she was known as Byrd. However, for me, she was Ma'Dear. Because of my great love for her, I named my first child after her. However, I did spare the child the full name.

When we were children, Ma'Dear kept us most of the time while my mother was work-in. She was there for most of the trials and tragedies in my life. She accepted my shortcomings, strengths, and weaknesses. Ma'Dear offered me, unconditional love. She never tried to change my behavior. It just wasn't her personality.

A merry heart doeth good like a medicine:
but a broken spirit drieth the bones.
Proverbs 17:22

Ma'Dear had a sense of humor that never faltered. There were many times that I was the recipient of her humor. She could turn any situation into a time of laughter. When we were children, we often thought her jokes were heartless. Whenever we would lose something, we would ask her the same question.

Inevitably, we would ask, "Ma'Dear, where is it at?"

Lil' Earline and Ms. Earline

She always responded the same way, "Behind the preposition at."

We would respond, "Ma'Dear, tell us where that's at!"

Roaring with laughter, she would again

respond, "Behind the preposition at!"

We didn't understand her answer. Therefore, we begged for help, "Ma'Dear p-l-e-a-s-e tell us where it's at!"

She never changed her answer, "Behind the preposition at."

Years later, we learned about prepositions in school. Even with this new knowledge, we were slow to understand the answer Ma'Dear had given us for so many years.

I recall all You have done, O LORD; I
remember Your wonderful deeds of long ago.
Psalm 77:11 NLT

Ma'Dear was usually mild mannered and accepting. That is unless you attacked one of her children. Instantly, another side of Ma'Dear would immerge. Whether the attack was mild or severe, Ma'Dear's response was going to be extreme.

Uncle Carlton and I began buying beer when we were in junior high school. He is Ma'Dear's youngest child, and he's three weeks older than me. The people who ran the neighborhood liquor store didn't seem to care about our age. At least, they never asked for identification. When it occurred to them to request identification, we were eighteen and had been purchasing alcoholic beverages from them for a number of years.

The crown of the wise is their riches: but the
foolishness of fools is folly.
Proverbs 14:24

One of the neighbors would send Carlton to the liquor store for her. She would give him a small sum of money for his efforts. One day, she accused Carlton of keeping her change. She had never seen Ma'Dear upset. Almost without warning, the docile Ma'Dear knocked her on the ground. Nearby, there was a brick lying on the ground. It didn't take much for Ma'Dear to grab it.

The blood of Christ will purify our hearts from deeds that lead to death so that we can worship the living God.
Hebrews 9:14 NLT

Aunt Pickle was standing nearby. She was able to stop the double tragedy, a tragedy for the woman and our family. As Ma'Dear aimed for the woman's head with the brick, Aunt Pickle grabbed Ma'Dear's arm. This was really ironic. Aunt Pickle was the real fighter in the family.

A few yards from this spot, another fight had once taken place. Aunt Pickle had beaten this same woman. She had stripped the woman's top off. Even now, it is hard to imagine Aunt Pickle breaking up a fight. It must have been God's grace.

He that loveth father or mother more than Me is not worthy of Me: and he that loveth son or daughter more than Me is not worthy of Me. **Matthew 10:37**

Mama told me another story about Ma'Dear. My mother has never been a fighter. As she was walking home from school, a group of children followed her. Mama was in the first or second grade. One of the girls was trying to start a fight with Mama. They were walking near the railroad tracks when Ma'Dear observed what was going on. Ma'Dear was the superhero, grabbing the child by the hand and slinging her to the other side of the railroad track. Again, God's grace kept Ma'Dear from being arrested.

Ma'Dear would never turn me away. It didn't matter what had happened. There were never any demands at her house. Ma'Dear was easygoing and very protective. I began to cleave to her. During the major tragedies in my life, my mother provided for all my material needs and Ma'Dear pitched in. Ma'Dear believed in sharing all of her material possessions. She denied herself of basic physical comforts to provide for the wants of her children.

I trusted Ma'Dear more than I trusted the banks. She was my personal banker. Actually, she could be trusted to hold everybody's money.

She was the example of love, humility, giving, and patience, in word and deed. She gave us something more precious than gold, the gift of laughter. She taught us to laugh at our mistakes, how to laugh at ourselves, and finally, how to laugh in the midst of sorrow. When Ma'Dear was diagnosed with Alzheimer's, she maintained her sense of humor. Whenever she would become confused, she would turn it into a joke. It was hard to tell if there was really something wrong with her.

I often wondered what I would do if something happened to Ma'Dear. The thought was too painful to bear. If Ma'Dear couldn't live forever, I preferred dying before her. I was sure that I would lose my mind if something happened to her.

You love Him even though you have never seen Him. Though you do not see Him, you trust Him; and even now you are happy with

*a glorious, inexpressible joy. Your reward for
trusting Him will be the salvation of your
souls.* **1 Peter 1:8-9 NLT**

After Mama became a Christian, she began
witnessing to Ma'Dear. Ma'Dear would listen
attentively. Afterward she would kneel at her chair.
Mama would lead her in reciting a sinner's prayer.
Periodically, Mama would return and this scene would
be repeated.

In 1999, it became difficult for Ma'Dear to
move around. She needed minor assistance with some
tasks. Our family thought she was suffering from
arthritis. She never complained about the pain or
discomfort.

Years before, Ma'Dear had fought a battle with
breast cancer. At the time, I was in junior high school.
After she was brought from the recovery room, our
family went to Ma'Dear's room. She was still sedated.
When Aunt Pickle walked over to her bedside, she
noticed Ma'Dear was missing something. She looked at
the nurse with alarm.

With her voice raised, she said, "Where are my
mother's teeth? That's not what the operation was for!"

The nurse responded calmly, "They are in the
drawer."

Although she had worn dentures for a number
of years, we didn't know that she had false teeth.
Ma'Dear found this amusing. This must have been a
good set of dentures. Even those who lived in the house
with Ma'Dear didn't know her secret. This shocked me
so much that I questioned everybody in our family. For
my efforts, I only found one person who knew
Ma'Dear's secret, her mother, Mae.

She recovered from the operation without complications. In subsequent years, she kept yearly appointments to monitor the status of the cancer. The tests were always negative.

God can use sorrow in our lives to help us
turn away from sin.
2 Corinthians 7:10 NLT

In December of 1999, the doctor decided to admit Ma'Dear to the hospital. They wanted to run some test. A few days before Christmas, we learned she had cancer again. When she was diagnosed with cancer for the second time, she showed no anger or resentment.

On Christmas Eve, the doctor operated on Ma'Dear. Cancer had spread to her liver. Our family camped out at the hospital all day. Christmas day was spent at the hospital with her. The children were glad to sacrifice our normal Christmas traditions and activities. We just wanted to be with Ma'Dear. She was sedated most of the time. Through all of this, she never complained about the pain. We looked at her face to determine when she was in need of pain medication.

I command thee this day to love the LORD thy
God, to walk in His ways, and to keep His
commandments and His statutes and His
judgments, that thou mayest live and multiply:
and the LORD thy God shall bless thee in the
land whither thou goest to posses it.
Deuteronomy 30:16

The doctors' diagnosis wasn't a favorable one. They estimated that Ma'Dear had less than six months to live. They suggested sending Ma'Dear to a hospice.

Things were moving too fast. It was hard for our family to accept so many negative reports at once.

My uncle made the decision. The doctors tried to get him to reconsider. My uncle was firm and adamant in his decision. There would be no hospice for Ma'Dear. She was going home. We would assist with her care. My uncle put his own life on hold to help care for his mother. This was a side of him that I had never seen. No task was too menial for him to perform.

The hospice staff monitored Ma'Dear's treatment. In the beginning, it appeared to the family that the diagnosis was wrong. Ma'Dear appeared to be getting better.

> *But they that wait upon the LORD shall*
> *renew their strength; they shall mount up*
> *with wings as eagles; they shall run, and not*
> *be weary; and they shall walk, and not faint.*
> **Isaiah 40:31**

At the hospital, Ma'Dear played with LaToya, bouncing a balloon across the room. She loved looking at LaToya. My daughter, Earline resembled Ma'Dear. LaToya is my only grandchild. The resemblance was magnified in LaToya. She's a younger replica of Ma'Dear.

When Ma'Dear returned home, her appetite was still good. She played video games with the grandchildren. One day, she got out of her hospital bed without assistance. She walked into the living room. She was concerned about my mother.

> *Yea, though I walk through the valley of the*
> *shadow of death, I will fear no evil: for Thou*
> *art with me; Thy rod and Thy staff they*

comfort me.
Psalm 23:4

When we brought Ma'Dear home from the hospital, her Bible was on the dresser in her room. We were surprised to find that it was opened to Psalm 23. The Psalm was marked and it was obvious that she had read this Psalm repeatedly. It didn't seem possible that Ma'Dear could be leaving us. Surely, the doctors had made a mistake. She seemed to be getting better.

A few days later, Mama had a dream. In the dream, she saw a beautiful fish. It looked so alive. When she walked over to the fish for a closer look, the fish was dead.

During the first week after her release from the hospital, Aunt Bobbie came down from Atlanta. She was Ma'Dear's younger sister. Aunt Bobbie was suffering with her own sickness. In addition to their sickness, Aunt Bobbie and Ma'Dear shared their sense of humor.

In the multitude of words there wanteth not sin: but he that refraineth his lips is wise.
Proverbs 10:19

When Aunt Bobbie arrived, Ma'Dear was sitting in a recliner in the living room. She looked up when her sister walked in. A smile crossed her face. Aunt Bobbie wanted to test Ma'Dear.

Jokingly, she said, "Byrd, do you know who I am?"

Laughingly, Ma'Dear replied, "Sure!"

Not willing to let it go at this, Aunt Bobbie asked, "Well who am I?"

Ma'Dear laughed, "You tell me!"

Each day before going to work, I stopped by to check on Ma'Dear. After my day was finished at work, I returned to stay with Ma'Dear. Her condition changed quickly. One morning, she appeared fine. When I returned eight hours later, it was obvious her condition had worsened. I requested time off from work to remain at her bedside. My mother had already taken family leave.

Having studied death and dying, I was acquainted with the symptoms of dying. It was obvious, her body shutting down. I was familiar with the grief process. Over the years, I had sat with a number of people in their last hours. Since I had experience in this area, I was ready for what was happening. At least, that's what I told myself. I asked the members of my family to release her. One by one, they came to say their farewells. It wasn't easy. It was hard for my uncle to accept her leaving.

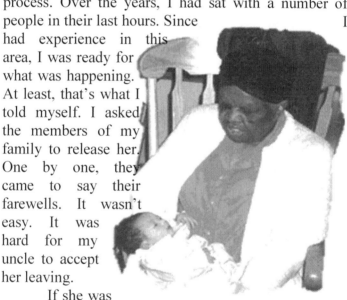

If she was going to leave, I wanted Ma'Dear to leave us peacefully and without worry for our welfare. I knew that she would be worried about her family. I said all the right things.

I instructed the family, "Reassure her that we are going to be alright. Tell her it's okay to leave us."

Let my mouth be filled with Thy praise and
with Thy honour all the day.
Psalm 71:8 NLT

Praise is important and essential to my life. Praise will help me get through almost any trial in my life. Therefore, I wanted to fill Ma'Dear's room with praise. It was a concert in her honor. As people came to visit her, I asked, "Can you sing?" If the answer was yes, I put in my request for them to sing.

And if it seem evil unto you to serve the
LORD, choose you this day whom ye will
serve; … but as for my house, and me we will
serve the LORD. Joshua 24:15

In between songs, I played a tape of Mama speaking at our former church. The tape was several years old. We had given Ma'Dear a copy of the message several years ago. Actually, we had given a copy of the tape to most of the unsaved members of our immediate family. Over the years, Ma'Dear had heard the tape numerous times. Now, the message had a renewed importance. The title of the message was *What Must I do to be Saved?*

For all the riches which God hath taken from
our father, that is ours, and our children's:
now then, whatsoever God hath said unto
thee, do. Genesis 31:16

One day, Mama told me she needed me to be praying about something. She was surprised. This wasn't a surprise for me. This had already occurred to me.

As I was standing in my bathroom, she made her secret request, "Don't tell anybody. I just want you to pray. I believe God wants me to do Ma'Dear's funeral."

As the days passed, the morphine didn't seem to be helping Ma'Dear's pain. She was requiring the medication with greater frequency and in larger doses. Ma'Dear's breathing pattern began to change. Mama and my uncle were in the living room. Uncle Carlton's birthday was the next day. As I watched her, I was scared she was going to pass on his birthday. That would be a hard memory for him.

Carlton was her youngest child. For most of his life, because of his disability, he lived with Ma'Dear. A few months earlier, he decided it was time for him to move out. He was concerned about his future. If something happened to Ma'Dear, his living arrangements would be uncertain. His fate would be determined by someone else. He made the choice without help from the family.

At Ma'Dear's bedside, I prayed, "God please don't let Ma'Dear pass on Carlton's birthday."

When I knew the time was drawing close, I called my mother and my uncle into the bedroom. There was no denying what was happening, Ma'Dear was leaving us. Within a few minutes, she took her last breath.

Don't be afraid, for I am with you. Do not be dismayed, for I am your God. I will strengthen you. I will help you. I will uphold you with My victorious right hand.
Isaiah 41:10 NLT

Ma'Dear passed on January 13, 2000, a month after she was diagnosed with Cancer for the second time. Mama was holding her right hand, while I held the left hand. My uncle was holding her feet. It was approximately an hour before Carlton's birthday. All of my brave preparations died with her. I was shocked. I couldn't believe that she had left me. The words that I had spoken to her were just that, words. I was never going to be all right without her.

> *Then Nehemiah the governor said to them, "Don't mourn or weep on such a day as this! For today is a sacred day before the LORD your God." For the people had all been weeping as they listened to the words of the Law. And Nehemiah continued, "Go and celebrate with a feast of rich foods and sweet drinks, and share gifts of food with people who have nothing prepared. This is a sacred day before our Lord. Don't be dejected and sad, for the joy of the LORD is your strength!"* **Nehemiah 8:9-10 NLT**

The next day, we began preparing for her homegoing celebration. Our family was unaware of the preparations that God had already put in place. Ma'Dear didn't have a church home. It had been years since her last visit to a church. In many ways, Mama had been her pastor. We were sitting in the kitchen at Ma'Dear's house preparing the obituary when the announcement was made.

My uncle asked, "Evelyn, who's going to do Ma'Dear's funeral, your pastor?"

She responded gently, "No."

Not satisfied with this answer, he asked, "Charlotte's pastor?"

Again, she responded, "No."

Running out of options, he asked, "Well who then, you?"

In an almost whispered voice, she responded, "Yes."

With relief and excitement, he responded, "Alright!"

I made plans for a family reunion. It was a day that I would remember for the rest of my life. It needed to be a beautiful day. I wanted it to be a glorious celebration of her life. God gave me more than I asked for. By His grace, He gave Mama the strength to conduct her first funeral. He was present throughout the service.

My granddaughter, La'Toya wrote a poem about her feeling for Ma'Dear. She read it at the funeral. The repast was a celebration that Ma'Dear would have enjoyed. It was a celebration of her life and legacy.

Blessed is the man that trusteth in the LORD,
and whose hope the LORD is.
Jeremiah 17:7

By God's grace, with time, the pain of Ma'Dear's loss has gotten better. Her memory and her legacy remain strong. Each time I drive past Warren Williams Apartments, I miss my grandmother. This is where she lived most of her life. Whenever I look at my granddaughter, I think of Ma'Dear.

There is only one thing that I wish I had said to her, "I'll see you in heaven!"

Chuck

But to all who believed Him and accepted Him, He gave the right to become children of God. They are reborn! This is not a physical birth resulting from human passion or plan -- this rebirth comes from God. John 1:12-13 NLT

Originally, I thought the second fire began with Jim, but perhaps, it was Chuck. While working at the Mayfair Lounge in my late teens, I met a pimp who was also a drug dealer, Jim (not his real name), who lived in Atlanta. Later, I became involved with him. It was a rocky relationship that lasted for more than ten years.

In some ways, my relationship with Jim ended when I met Buck. I was vulnerable when I met him. I had wanted a good and solid relationship for years. He came along during one of the crisis periods in my life, after a bad Jim experience.

The night I became involved with Buck, I was planning on going to the H & D, a club in Phenix City, with a friend and Jim's sister, Reba. This very popular club stayed open late. It was always packed. We had all planned to wear red dresses. Jim knew this was our plan. He had another plan.

When I arrived to pick his sister up, my cousin was there with her boyfriend. Reba informed me she wasn't going with us because Jim was planning to take someone else to the same club. She said that she didn't want to be in the middle of our mess. After I assured her there would be no trouble, she agreed to go to the club. This marked the last time that Jim was able to inflict pain in my heart.

Who hath put wisdom in the inward parts? or who hath given understanding to the heart?
Job 38:36

When Jim found out about my relationship with Buck, he assumed this was something that would pass and he was still in control. Jim had vowed to wait for

Buck to violate our relationship. He was sure it was only matter of time before Buck took me for granted. A year after my breakup with Jim, I married Buck. Jim kept his promise to wait for Buck to mess up.

Jim was part of my past. In many ways, he was my past. Chuck was his father. During many difficult periods in my life, he became my substitute father. For many years, Chuck had been a part of my life. After my relationship ended with Jim, Chuck continued to be an important part of my life. In fact, my relationship with

Jim had taken so many turns during the years that everyone in his family had become my family. Chuck pushed me to end my relationship with his son. He also pushed me to do something positive with my life. When it appeared I was finally headed in the right direction, Chuck was happy for me. From afar, he was often silently cheering me on. I always knew that he was there if I needed him.

Chuck was reliable and dependable. After I ended my relationship with Jim, it wasn't a necessity for me to rely on him. There was security in knowing that he was there if I needed him. There had been times when the need had been an almost constant occurrence. After I recommitted my life to the Lord, the need became less frequent.

After I left the streets, I seldom saw Chuck. He wanted it that way. He encouraged me to stay away from East Wynnton. He also encouraged me to stay away from his son, Jim. In the past, both had caused me problems. He was concerned they would suck me back into the lifestyle. Both had the potential to burn me badly.

Will a man rob God? Yet ye have robbed Me. But ye say, Wherein have we robbed Thee? In tithes and offerings. Ye are cursed with a curse: for ye have robbed Me, even this whole nation. Bring ye all the tithes into the storehouse, that there may be meat in mine house, and prove me now herewith, saith the Lord of hosts if I will not open you the windows of heaven, and pour you out a blessing, that there shall not be room enough to receive it. And I will rebuke the devourer

for your sakes, and he shall not destroy the
fruits of your ground; neither shall your vine
cast her fruit before the time in the field,
saith the Lord of hosts. And all nations shall
call you blessed: for ye shall be a delightsome
land, saith the Lord of hosts.
Malachi 3: 8-12

It had been a long time since I had seen Chuck. Occasionally, I attended services at a church across the street from his home. During these times, I would stop by Chuck's house. It had been a long time since I visited this church. Therefore, it had been a long time since I visited Chuck.

I was in one of the back rooms of my house when I heard a voice speak.

The voice said clearly, "When was the last time you saw Chuck?"

Without hesitation, I responded, "It's been a while."

The voice responded, "Go by his house and get an offering for the church."

Without considering who was speaking to me, I answered, "I don't believe in asking people for donations to the church. The church is supposed to be supported by tithes and offerings."

I was confident of something that I had heard from my daughter, Earline. She often said, "Where God guides, He provides. Where He leads, He proceeds."

And I will see to it that the Egyptians treat
you well. They will load you down with gifts
so you will not leave empty-handed.
Exodus 3:21

God is able to provide for any ministry that He establishes. Begging sinners for donations, selling barbecue ribs and chicken, and robbing God's people were not what I considered provision. God is looking for willing sacrifices. He also wants us to receive those sacrifices with thanksgiving and gladness of heart.

> *The blessing of the LORD makes a person*
> *rich, and He adds no sorrow with it.*
> **Proverbs 10:22 NLT**

During my time in the streets, I had observed or participated in many con or confidence games. This is a game of taking advantage of someone because of their greed or a desire for material wealth. You promised people things that you knew were appealing to them. It only requires a small investment from them to receive a greater reward or return on their investment. In other words, you appeal to the person's greed by offering them something for nothing. There were many things about money schemes or get-rich tricks that concerned me. God already knew how strongly I felt about church finances, why would He ask me to do this?

Patiently, He responded, "You haven't seen him in a while. Go by to see him."

> *And the Lord called Samuel again the third*
> *time. And he arose and went to Eli, and said,*
> *Here am I; for thou didst call me. And Eli*
> *perceived that the Lord had called the child.*
> *Therefore Eli said unto Samuel, Go, lie*
> *down: and it shall be if He call thee, that*
> *thou shalt say, Speak, Lord; for Thy servant*
> *heareth.* **1 Samuel 3:8-9**

It was a brief conversation. It ended before I had time to return to the den. My mother was sitting in the den. Before I processed what had happened, I shared the conversation with my mother. It reminded her of a similar conversation that she had with God. She encouraged me to call Chuck. Immediately, I went to make the telephone call. The telephone rang several times, but there was no answer. The conversation with God was pushed from my mind.

The next day, my mother and I were again sitting in the den. The voice came a second time.

"Go by Chuck's (not the real name God used) and get an offering for the church."

In those days was Hezekiah sick unto death. And the prophet Isaiah the son of Amoz came to him, and said unto him, Thus saith the LORD, Set thine house in order; for thou shalt die, and not live.
2 Kings 20:1

Instantly, I shared this message with my mother. At this point, I didn't argue with God, as I had on the previous day. Immediately, I made the telephone call. This time, his grandson answered the telephone. After a brief conversation, he gave the telephone to Chuck.

There was no need to identify myself to Chuck. He had known my voice for many years.

Anxiously, I asked, "Chuck, how are you doing?"

I wasn't prepared for his answer. A very weak voice responded, "Charlotte, I'm not doing so well."

Chuck was never one to complain. At once, I knew something was wrong.

I replied, "Before the week is out, I'm coming to see you."

With a voice that almost whispered, he responded, "Okay."

My mother had been listening.

As I hung up the telephone, she told me, "You need to go now."

Her comment was almost a command. Fear gripped my heart. What was wrong with Chuck?

Not sure that I could handle this alone, I answered, "You'll have to go with me."

If we confess our sins to Him, He is faithful
and just to forgive us.
1 John 1:9 NLT

It took us less than five minutes to dress and leave the house. Chuck's apartment was less than ten minutes away. We made the drive in silence. The neighborhood was familiar to me. There were always people sitting outdoors on their porches. I didn't notice their faces. When we arrived at the apartment, my fear almost turned to panic. I parked my car in front of his door. There was a sign posted on the front door.

"No smoking! Oxygen in use."

His condition was serious. As I knocked, I opened the door. His grandson was sitting in the living room and pointed me towards the bedroom. As I walked past him, he headed out the front door. My mother followed me into the bedroom.

Over the years, I had been to this apartment numerous times. I knew it well. Chuck was lying in his bed. His thin frail frame looked up at me, as I tried to hold back my tears. Gently, I sat down on the bed next to him.

The words were almost mumbled as they left my mouth, "What's wrong?"

The weak voice responded, "Charlotte, it's the cancer. It doesn't look good."

Years before, Chuck had fought a battle with cancer. After the previous battle, it was necessary for him to use a voice box. For years, by God's grace, the cancer had been in remission. Now, cancer had returned with a vengeance. No longer able to hold them back, the tears broke from my eyes.

> *So everywhere we go, we tell everyone about*
> *Christ. We warn them and teach them with*
> *all the wisdom God has given us.*
> **Colossians 1:28a NLT**

Between my continuous sobs, I almost begged him; "You have to give your life to the Lord. I don't think I can handle it if you don't. It would worry me forever. "

> *That if thou shalt confess with thy mouth the*
> *Lord Jesus, and shalt believe in thine heart*
> *that God hath raised Him from the dead,*
> *thou shalt be saved. For with the heart man*
> *believeth unto righteousness; and with the*
> *mouth confession is made unto salvation.*
> **Romans 10:9-10**

As I continued to cry, Mama anointed his head with oil. She also explained to him God's plan of salvation. When she finished, Chuck told us he wanted to be alone to talk with God. After being sure he understood the need for salvation, I assured him that I would be back the next day. It was something I needed to do for me. I needed to know for my peace of mind. I needed to know that he had accepted God's grace.

The next day, I stopped by Chuck's home after leaving work. He assured me that he had talked with God. Chuck further assured me that in his prayer he had repented for his sins. During the next days, his appetite diminished and his health declined rapidly.

Late one night, I got a call from his daughter, Reba. Reba and I had been friends for years. She was at the hospital. She wanted me to come. As I rushed across town, I was barely able to see the cars around me. My tears clouded my eyes, but the traffic flow was light.

The LORD gives His people strength. The LORD blesses them with peace.
Psalm 29:1

The end was near for Chuck. I prayed that he wouldn't leave. When I arrived at the hospital, Reba was in the family waiting room with her mother. I learned he was already gone. Reba didn't want to tell me over the telephone. A nurse took me back to the room where Chuck was being held. He was lying on a table. I kissed him goodbye, as my tears washed over his face.

I followed Reba when we left the hospital. Shortly after that, we arrived at Chuck's home. Reba gave me my second shock for the night.

As if she had already planned it, she told me, "I want you to speak at Chuck's funeral."

She wasn't really asking me. This was Reba. She never really asked anything. It was understood; I would do it. It was something Chuck would want me to do. In spite of this fact, I wasn't sure I could handle the task.

But my God shall supply all your need according to His riches in glory by Christ Jesus. **Philippians 4:19**

For several days, I wondered what I would say at his funeral. Chuck told me that he had repented for his sins. There had been no time for him to develop his relationship with Christ. I wanted to say the right things. Assurance was what I needed. I needed to be assured that Chuck had indeed found salvation.

My soul longeth, yea, even fainteth for the courts of the LORD: my heart and my flesh crieth out for the living God. **Psalm 84:2**

The morning of the funeral, I awoke to the sound of music flowing from my lips. It was such a beautiful song. It had never meant so much to me as on this day.

In my dream, I had heard the song. "It is well. It is well with my soul."

It finally hit me. I had collected the offering for the church. The real offering is a soul, a living sacrifice. And I can say with assurance, "I'll see you in heaven."

Aunt Bobbie

***Many waters cannot quench love, neither can the
floods drown it: if a man would give all the substance
of his house for love, it would utterly be contemned.***
Song of Solomon 8:7 NIV

Barbara Owens Morgan Eberhart had been a
part of my life even before my birth. At this time of my
birth, Aunt Bobbie didn't have any children. She had
already developed an attachment to the child my
mother was carrying. This night would serve to make
the attachment worse. In the coming years, she would
be overly concerned about everything I did. She would
constantly remind me of one thing.

"You were supposed to be my baby."

She never forgot to tell me this and I never
forgot I had another mother watching everything I did.
Before I was born, Mama had promised to give me to
Aunt Bobbie and her husband. After seeing me, Mama
decided to keep her baby. During her pregnancy, Mama
was overly embarrassed because she wasn't married.
As her pregnancy advanced, she had worn an overcoat
whenever she ventured outdoors. She was attempting to
hide the growing bulge in her waste. At least, this is the
way Aunt Bobbie told the story. She also remembered
Mama crying out the night she was in labor.

According to Aunt Bobbie, Mama screamed,
"Lord, I want to run, but where can I hide?"

Shortly after I turned twenty-one years old, I
sustained second and third-degree burns to seventy
percent of my body. This resulted from an incident of

domestic violence. That was several years before I met Buck. At the time, I was living in Atlanta, Georgia. After I was admitted to intensive care, my aunt was the first family member that I remembered seeing. When my Mama entered my hospital room the first time, she was with my Aunt Bobbie.

Whatever you do, you must do all for the glory of God. 1 Corinthians 10:31 NLT

My aunt is a real comedian and even in my pain, she wanted me to laugh. She told me that when she was told about what had happened to me, she ran to the car. There was only one problem. She was running so fast that she missed the car. She slid beneath the car and had to be pulled from under the car. Prior to her accident, Aunt Bobbie had been drinking, but she was sober when she told me the story. This began a continuous routine of them visiting me. These two people were the only ones to weather the storm.

Aunt Bobbie came several times a day, for almost three months, until the nurses asked her to skip a day. They said that I was getting too dependent on her.

Go away, all you who do evil, for the LORD has heard my crying. Psalms 6:8 NLT

On several occasions, during this time period, Mama and Aunt Bobbie went to the family waiting room and cried together. Unable to ring the buzzer to request the assistance of a nurse, my almost continuous cries for help were sometimes interpreted as complaining. To avoid this, my aunt began to provide most of my routine care. Arriving at the hospital before breakfast, she would ensure that I was fed with care and in a timely manner. She would leave the hospital allowing just enough time to arrive at her job at the appointed time. In the evenings, she would return from work to feed me my dinner.

Scraping the Silvadine ointment from the wounds also required a lot of patience to avoid hurting me. After several bad experiences with this, I was afraid for most of the nurses to touch me. Some of the nurses that were assigned to care for me seemed impatient to get the cream changed. In their hastiness, they caused me immense pain. My Aunt Bobbie requested permission to perform this task, too. There was no way to alleviate all the pain associated with this procedure, but at least she made every effort not to unnecessarily hurt me. After I was released from the hospital, I moved back to Columbus, Georgia.

Years later, when I was arrested for selling drugs, Aunt Bobbie was there. The first day of my trial, Aunt Bobbie was in the courtroom with me. She encouraged me to leave town to avoid going to prison. I didn't want to run for the rest of my life. Therefore, I decided that I would tough it out. Nevertheless, the thought of going to prison was repulsive to me.

Now we see things imperfectly as in a poor

***mirror, but then we will see everything with
perfect clarity. All that I know now is partial
and incomplete, but then I will know
everything completely.***
1 Corinthians 13:12 NLT

Several years ago, Aunt Bobbie's health began to decline. There was one diagnosis after another one, high blood pressure, sugar diabetes, renal failure, Lupus, and finally cancer. No matter the diagnosis, she kept fighting. She refused to be downhearted or give in to the sickness.

Aunt Bobbie was still residing in Atlanta. My mother began calling her several times a day. During every telephone call, she wanted to know where I was, what I was doing, where Herman was, where Earline was, and what they were doing. Sometimes, I found this intrusive and irritating. I never told her how I felt.

Whenever Mama felt a need to see Aunt Bobbie, I drove her to Atlanta. Mama was constantly thanking her for all the things she had done to help me. Aunt Bobbie didn't want the continuous "thank you." She had her own reasons for helping me. She had the special attachment for me. It was the attachment that vexed me for many years, often to the point of frustration. That same attachment encouraged her to meddle in my life on numerous occasions.

***He replied, "What is impossible from a
human perspective is possible with God."***
Luke 18:27 NLT

For a number of years, Aunt Bobbie had worked at a dialysis clinic. When it became necessary for her to be the recipient of the same services that she had assisted so many others with, she wasn't amused. She found all thoughts of dialysis repulsive. She reluctantly consented to the treatments. These proved difficult and tedious. There were persistent complications with the treatments. After several hospital confinements, she informed her doctors that she was discontinuing dialysis. She was determined to have it her way. There was nothing to discuss.

> *When Jesus heard it, He saith unto them,*
> *They that are whole have no need of the*
> *physician, but they that are sick: I came not*
> *to call the righteous, but sinners to*
> *repentance.* **Mark 2:17**

Aunt Bobbie continued the treatment for the other conditions that were attacking her health. However, for months, there was no dialysis. It was difficult for her to eat more than a few morsels of food without severe abdominal pain. She came to Columbus several times to spend time with my mother. Mama cooked the foods that Aunt Bobbie was craving. During her visits to my home, she was able to rest and eat.

When my first book was released, Aunt Bobbie came to Columbus to support me. She spent an entire day with me in preparations for my first book signing. She was so excited that she was given a reprieve from the pain. She purchased numerous copies of the books for her friends. She was the best salesperson. We later learned the secret to her sales' technique.

This was her sales' pitch, "My niece wrote a book and I want you to buy one. I got your copy."

Your attitude should be the same that Christ

***Jesus had. Though He was God, He did not
demand and cling to His rights as God.*
Philippians 2:5-6 NLT**

During her many trips to the hospital, she sold my books. She kept the books displayed in her room. Whenever she went for a doctor's visit or any other appointment, she took my books with her. Later, it was necessary for her to carry a portable oxygen tank with her. This didn't hinder her. She continued to be extremely independent.

When I began planning a trip to Florida that would last for several days, she began making plans to go with me. This bothered me, but I didn't know how to handle it. I didn't want to hurt her feelings, but I was afraid that she would get sicker during the trip. She told me the trip was cleared by her doctors.

A few days before my departure, Aunt Bobbie's health took a turn for the worse. One morning, my daughter, Earline was listening to the radio. She heard that a famous author was having a book signing in Atlanta. We decided to travel to Atlanta for the signing. While we were at the bookstore, Mama would have an opportunity to visit Aunt Bobbie.

After we arrived at my aunt's home in Atlanta, one of her friends called the house. I answered the telephone. She asked me to observe my aunt closely. It was obvious that she was having difficulty breathing. The oxygen tank wasn't supplying enough oxygen. I called her doctor and discovered she had no knowledge of our trip to Florida. An ambulance had to be called to take Aunt Bobbie to the hospital. Her only obvious concern was that she would miss the trip to Florida.

While in Florida, we called Aunt Bobbie several

times a day. One day, we learned that she had been moved to intensive care. The morning after we returned to Columbus, I received a telephone call. Aunt Bobbie wanted to see my mother. She was also giving her jewelry away. Within an hour, we were headed to Atlanta.

> *As the time of his death drew near, he called for his son Joseph and said to him, "If you are pleased with me, swear most solemnly that you will honor this, my last request: Do not bury me in Egypt.*
> **Genesis 47:29 NLT**

When we arrived at the hospital, Aunt Bobbie was coherent. In her room in intensive care, she had several of my books on display. When I attempted to move them, she stopped me.

In her usual obstinate manner, she demanded, "Leave my books alone! I have some money for you. I'm expecting one of my friends to bring me some more."

The day that she allowed me to remove the books, I knew the end was near. For two days, members of our family visited with her around the clock. We were living in a small area outside her room. When she found herself alone for two minutes, she slipped quietly away. Even in death, she was determined to do it her own way.

For several years, Aunt Bobbie had been planning her funeral. She wanted to be buried in a purple casket in a purple suit. Instead of flowers, she wanted lots of balloons. She also made out the program and the obituary. At her funeral, she wanted the praise dancers to dance. The funeral celebration was to be a reflection of her unique personality.

Over the years, we had spent numerous nights at Aunt Bobbie's house. Atlanta would never be the same without her. We drove to Atlanta for her funeral. It wasn't quite the way she had planned it; however, it was a tribute that she would have enjoyed.

Jim

***Yea, I have loved thee with an everlasting
love: therefore in love and kindness have I
drawn thee.***
Jeremiah 31:3b

When Chuck passed, Jim was in prison. He was

scheduled for release on parole at that time. There was a delay with his release papers. Therefore, he missed Chuck's funeral. It had been years since I had seen or heard from Jim. My heart went out to him. This must be really hard for him. I didn't need to see him to know that he was in pain. There was no need to talk to him. There was something else I knew about him; he would deny the pain.

There was a bond between Jim and me. It was a bond that had never been challenged. It had never been broken. It was a

soul tie. Neither of us held out any hope for a future together. In spite of this, there remained an invisible attachment that we both knew existed. It wasn't something that we wanted or flamed. It was simply there. It had been there since I was eighteen. During the last fifteen years, we had barely seen each other. Yet, the bond remained.

I am the favorite topic of town gossip, and all the drunkards sing about me.
Psalms 69:12

A month after Chuck's passing, Jim was released from prison. He was released to reside in Columbus with his mother. Over the years, Jim had kept abreast of my activities, as well as those of my now ex-husband, Buck. This time was no different. He knew that Buck was in prison again. He also knew that we had been divorced for several years and that I wasn't dating. Most of all, he knew that I was saved. The soul tie stirred up and he thought it was a perfect opportunity.

The night he came home from prison, he called me. He was staying with his mother. He stated that he had begun to develop a relationship with God during his incarceration. This was something that he was proud of. It had been years since we had seen each other. He asked me to come over to his mother's house. After making sure, we wouldn't be alone, I agreed. This was worth seeing. On more than one occasion, I had witnessed to Jim. His response was never forgotten.

When arguing with fools, don't answer their foolish arguments, or you will become as foolish as they are. When arguing with fools, be sure to answer their foolish arguments, or they will become wise in their own estimation. Trusting a fool to convey a message is as foolish as cutting off one's feet or drinking poison! **Proverbs 26:4-6**

He would respond rudely, "Don't bring that at me. I'm going to hell where the party will be going on night and day. There will be plenty of freaks and plenty of cocaine."

When I arrived at the house, I was careful to keep my distance from him. When he attempted to greet me with a kiss, I made sure it landed on my cheek. His mother was watching television in the living room. We stayed in the room with her. I sat on the sofa with her.

During his incarceration, Jim had spent a lot of time reading the Word. We talked about the Bible. He had countless tapes, which he had accumulated during his sentence. Some of them were powerful sermons. It seemed he had almost memorized them. He was eager to share them with me. Jim knew which tapes would minister to me. He didn't know the type of music that I liked. He preferred music that had a rhythm that reminded me of what I enjoyed before my salvation. My preference is for praise and worship music. He had an abundant supply of both kinds of music.

Shortly after my arrival, his parole officer stopped by the house. It didn't take much for him to vex me. As Jim began to tell him about his conversion, the officer assured him that he had heard it all before. He had made one assumption, "It never lasts."

He that believeth on Me, as the scripture hath said, out of his belly shall flow rivers of living water. **John 7:38**

I wasn't sure about Jim's salvation; however, there were two things that I was certain of. My salvation was genuine and the officer needed Jesus as much I did. He needed Jesus as much as Jim did. I didn't hesitate in sharing this information with him.

Over the next few weeks, Jim and I went to several churches together. The interaction between us was a pleasant diversion. His company was enjoyable.

The soul ties kept the fantasy going. Jim often joked about us getting married. It was just the soul ties speaking. The truth was that we enjoyed aggravating each other. Although there was no desire for a romantic future together, we enjoyed reminiscing about the mistakes of the past. There were some things that I considered taboo. These were things that we needed to leave unspoken.

The first week he was home, I knew one thing about him hadn't changed. He was still a hustler. He tried unsuccessfully to hustle me the first week. After a trip to a church, we stopped at a car wash. Jim helped me wash the car. As we were drying the car, he stuck his foot in his mouth.

In the tone of the old Jim, he said, "I helped you wash your car; you should give me the money to pay my parole fee!"

Laughing, I responded, "What?"

When it became clear that I was not going to give him the thirty bucks, he stopped helping me with the car. If he had simply asked me for the money, my answer may have been different.

The Charlotte that Jim remembered was dead. He didn't know how to relate to the new one. Jim had always been focused on his personal needs. This allowed very little time to focus on the needs of others. He had known me for years; yet, he didn't know me at all. He tried to remind me of the things that I liked. There was one problem; he had never taken the time to discover my likes and dislikes. He had been too absorbed in himself. Yet, the soul tie remained.

Jim was out of touch with who I was as a person. This made me wonder if Buck knew me at all. Jim had known me longer than Buck had known me. I needed to visit Buck. My divorce from Buck had been final for some time. It had been several months since I had seen him. He was serving time at a prison in South Georgia. The gossip mill would let him know that I was spending time with Jim. I wanted to be the first one to tell him.

As surely as a wind from the north brings
rain, so a gossiping tongue causes anger!
Proverbs 25:23

When I informed him of Jim's release, Buck wasn't surprised. News always travels fast through the prison grapevine. He knew the time of his release was getting closer. However, he was confused about the nature of my relationship with Jim.

Whenever Buck was messing up, Jim was always there. He was out of site, but he was always popping up in our relationship. When I became involved with Buck, Jim promised that he would never go away quietly. This was a promise that he kept. It was hard for me to explain. While I did not intend to have a romantic relationship with Jim, he was very much a part of my life.

Buck and I decided to give our relationship

another try. When I returned home from my visit with Buck, I told Jim I was planning to reconcile with Buck. That didn't disturb him. He thought I was making another mistake. Although Jim joked about us getting married, he knew it wasn't meant to be. It was just the soul tie acting up. Jim continued to call me. He said that he would stop when Buck came home from prison. Until that time, he planned to continue aggravating me. I planned to return the favor. He was also calling the other women from his past.

When I decided to write *A Journey to Hell and Back,* I found support from both Buck and Jim. In fact, Jim was proud of the book. Immediately, he began to promote the book on his job.

This was his assessment, "You told a nice version. It was much worse than what you said. I was worse than what was said, so were your husbands. You could have used my real name."

During this time, Jim's daughter, Selene was serving time in prison. Shortly after the book was released, she was released from prison and briefly visited Columbus. When Jim continued to ask me about marriage, I told him that he would have to get permission from Selene.

One night, I went to Reba's house (Jim's sister) to visit Selene. It had been several months since I had seen Reba. She was standing at the stove cooking. She was an excellent cook. Although Reba had lost a lot of weight, I didn't comment. Reba was never at a loss for a sharp retort. This time was no different.

With her usual sarcasm, she chided, "The only time we see you is when Selene is in town."

I responded, "I didn't know you wanted to see

me."

I had no idea how true my words were. Later, I discovered Reba had been seriously ill. When Selene walked into the kitchen, I continued with the purpose of my visit. Selene had also been sick for some time. My concern for her health was the reason for my visit. When I saw her, I knew my concern was justified. I tried to control my facial expression. We spent the next day checking the status of her health. I told her about the conversations with Jim.

She was adamant; "He doesn't have worry about me ever agreeing to that. He may have changed, but I wouldn't want you to risk it. I don't think he can convince me. Go back to Buck. You can work with him."

She had her own reason for drawing this conclusion. Selene didn't hesitate to share them with me. Shortly after this time, Selene left town and it was months before I saw her again. However, we continued to call each other.

> *[Satan] prowls around like a roaring lion,*
> *looking for some victim to devour. Take a*
> *firm stand against him, and be strong in your*
> *faith*. **1 Peter 5:8-9 NLT**

Several weeks later, I received a troubling telephone call. As I was walking through a local bookstore, my cell phone rang. It was one of my cousins. She had some news for me. I thought it was about Selene. It wasn't. It was about Reba. She had passed away and I didn't even know that she was sick. Her heart had failed while she was sleeping in her bed.

Selene came back for the funeral. There was

one problem; Columbus had always caused her problems. After the funeral, we couldn't get her to leave Columbus. Being here wasn't good for her health. Friends and bad habits threatened to destroy her. There were several trips to the hospital. One night, as I was taking her to the hospital, I called Jim. I asked him to meet us at the local emergency room. Selene was so scared. She was his daughter. Yet, he refused to come. His insensitivity hurt me. After we arrived at the emergency room, I called him again. I was almost begging him to come.

> *He that is slow to anger is better than the mighty; and he that ruleth his spirit than he that taketh a city.* **Proverbs 16:32**

Angrily, he screamed at me, "I'm not coming! I tried to get her to go last night, but she wouldn't go."

This was the first time that he had raised his voice at me in years. He could be snappy and stubborn. In spite of this, he was usually careful not to raise his voice with me. When I finished talking to him, I told Selene that was the last straw. He didn't have anything else to say to me. In a few days, Selene was released from the hospital. She went back to her bad habits.

> *All his days also he eateth in darkness, and he hath much sorrow and wrath with his sickness.* **Ecclesiastes 5:17**

The next time I heard from Selene, my mother, my granddaughter, and I were traveling down the highway in Atlanta, Georgia. I was scheduled to speak at a church within a few minutes. My cell phone rang and I answered it.

Tearfully, Selene said, "Charlotte, Daddy's dead!"

Shocked, I responded, "Daddy who?"

"Daddy! Daddy!"

"No, he's not!"

"Yes, he is Charlotte!"

"How can he be dead?"

"He died a few minutes ago at Auntie Reba's house."

So they sat down with him upon the ground seven days and seven nights, and none spake a word unto him: for they saw that his grief was very great. **Job 2:13**

We drove on to the church. There was no time to grieve. There was no time for tears. I had to bring a message of encouragement. I was only a couple of blocks from the church. God's grace helped me bring the message. My plans for the evening were changed; I drove back to Columbus that night. As I drove, I remembered countless memories that I had shared with Jim in Atlanta.

Then when Jacob had finished this charge to his sons, he lay back in the bed, breathed his last, and died. **Genesis 49:33 NLT**

When I arrived in Columbus, I went straight to Reba's house. It was exactly one month since Reba had passed. It was the same house. It was a different bed, but the same method. His heart had failed.

He will give you all you need from day to day if you live for Him and make the Kingdom of

God your primary concern.
Matthew 6:33 NLT

There were so many things to be sorry for. Our last words had been angry. Over the years, there had been numerous arguments about Selene. There had been arguments about numerous things. After a period of time, the arguments always faded away. This time, there would be no amends, no, I'm sorry. There wouldn't be time to straighten things out. It was too late for me to take back my last words to him.

Things were happening too quickly. I hadn't adjusted to Reba's death. Now, there was something else I needed to deal with.

My feelings about Jim had always been confusing. This would be no different. There was still that soul tie. We were friends who made the mistake of sharing something sacred. We became intimate and created a bond between us that neither of us seemed able or willing to break.

When I was twenty, we spent two weeks alone in Harlem. Money was coming in so slowly it was almost invisible. In a way we never had before, we depended on each other. Sometimes, we shared only five dollars to provide food for the day. There was something endearing in a person sharing the last piece of bologna with you. It was my first time being that far from home. I was in a city filled with strangers, hustling strangers.

It was a time when I really needed Jim. He was there for me. At least, he was there for the first two weeks of our trip. After the two weeks, he was the same old Jim. He started his tricks. I became angry with him.

We resided in different parts of the city temporarily. Eventually, I relented and moved near him.

There were times when I had wanted a relationship with Jim and he didn't want one with me. Later, he wanted a relationship with me and I didn't want one with him. It gave me a strange sense of satisfaction to see our roles reversed. In the midst of the confusion, it always bothered me to see him with someone else. It bothered him to see me with anyone else. We often laughed about this foolishness. The attachment defied logic. It defied reason.

> *Even my best friend, the one I trusted completely, the one who shared my food, has turned against me.* **Psalms 41:9 NLT**

Romantically, I was no longer attracted to Jim. After the first few weeks of our original relationship, I never trusted him again. In fact, there were times I found him to be the most unscrupulous person that I had ever met. There had been more than once when my life had been in jeopardy because of his antics. Even after he confessed salvation, I often found conversations with him tedious. He was still stubborn. None of these things stopped the connection between us.

One of us would become irritated in almost every conversation. Inevitably, in a few days, he would call me again. These calls were more to aggravate me than to communicate with me.

Whenever I answered the telephone, it started the same way. With a high pitch in his voice, he would say, "Charlotte Hall where is my mother-in-law? I don't want to talk to you!"

How I hated that name. Jim laughed at my irritation. He refused to call me Charlotte Johnson. Jim preferred to call me by the name that I carried when he met me. It was also a way of minimized my marriage to Buck. It was also his way of reminding me of my first husband, Robert. My current last name was a thorn in his flesh. Now, there would be no more irritating telephone calls. I had grown accustomed to the irritation and the aggravation.

Over the years, there had been numerous separations, most of them without a simple goodbye. Inevitably, in a few months or a few years, he would drop into my life again. Now, he was gone from my life forever.

***And you must love the LORD your God with all your heart, all your soul, and all your strength* Deuteronomy 6:5 NLT**

Even in his death, he took something from me that was never meant to be given to him, a piece of my soul. Time had failed to sever the invisible bond between us. Now, death had failed to sever it. Our failure to resolve our relationship and feelings had lingered for too long. For years, we had been enmeshed in each other's lives.

I tried not to think about him. In spite of my best intentions, even in death, he continued to pull at my soul. It was better to push him from my mind. At least, I tried.

In The Beginning

As for God, His way is perfect: the word of the LORD is tried: He is a buckler to all those that trust in Him. **Psalm 18:30**

When Buck and I got married the first time, I wanted to be the Proverbs kind of wife. I just never saw this example. Our marriage started crazy from the beginning. We both felt pressured to get married because it was obvious I was going to prison. Buck was out of prison on parole. During his incarceration, I had been arrested on drug-related charges. In the midst of my criminal trial on these charges, it became apparent that I was going to prison.

The State of Georgia has strict rules about relationships between ex-felons. We knew it would be a problem for us to continue our relationship with me in prison and him on parole. Eventually, there would be two parole officers monitoring our lives. During the court recess, Buck and I were married.

The judge gave me a fifteen-year sentence for the possession of cocaine and ten years for the possession of marijuana. Both sentences would run concurrently He had given me the maximum sentence for the charge.

We had a very unusual honeymoon. I spent the first two weeks of the honeymoon in jail without my husband. We were able to communicate regularly through the mail. Before the end of the month, my new husband joined me for the honeymoon. However, he was not coming to share my suite. There was a separate suite reserved for him, with his name on it.

> *Let him that stole steal no more: but*
> *rather let him labour, working with his hands*
> *the thing which is good, that he may have to*
> *give to him that needeth.*
> **Ephesians 4:28**

After I was locked up, Buck's stealing sprees escalated. His drug addiction was driving his behavior. Although I begged him to stop, he increased both habits, stealing and getting high. His arrest was inevitable.

After his arrest, Buck was assigned to the fifth floor and I was housed on the third floor of the Muscogee County Jail. He was assigned to the cellblock that was directly two floors above my cellblock. There are three cellblocks on each floor. Inside each cellblock, there were two levels surrounding a central day room. The day room also served as the dining area. There were several metal picnic style table sets in each day room. From the day room, there are stairs leading upstairs and downstairs to each level. There were approximately eight cells (rooms) on each floor of the cellblock. Each room had a metal twin bed, a metal sink that was connected to the toilet, and a vinyl mattress. There was also a door to each room. If the door closed, you were locked inside your room until a guard released you. The doors were usually locked to confine the inmates who committed some infraction inside the jail. There was a small flap near the bottom of each door. It was large enough to slide a tray of food through.

By giving another inmate some store goods, Buck arranged to secure the room directly above my room. It wasn't an ideal arrangement. However, we were able to make the best of a bad situation.

The Muscogee County Jail had a unique communication system. The toilets were connected between the floors. If you pumped the water out of the toilet and disinfected the toilet with Comet, the toilet could serve as a telephone. The newspaper could be used to make a kind of makeshift horn. The horn extended from the toilet allowing your voice to travel through the newspaper and through the pipes. Thus, you were able to talk to inmates housed on other floors of the jail. This was how we spent our honeymoon, bent over the toilet talking to each other.

> *For I hate divorce!" says the LORD, the God*
> *of Israel. "It is as cruel as putting on a*
> *victim's bloodstained coat," says the LORD*
> *Almighty. "So guard yourself; always remain*
> *loyal to your wife."*
> **Malachi 2:16 NLT**

When I met Buck, he was addicted to heroin and cocaine. This was hard to accept, but when he began abusing crack, it was impossible to accept. This started another cycle in our lives. I had been desperate to marry him. Now, I was desperate to divorce him. The heroin addiction offered some hope. I knew heroin had a bottom out cycle (a point a user would no longer desire the drug). An addict would reach this point if they lived long enough.

Crack was different. The drug causes rapid aging and deterioration of the body. The smell of the drug is horrible. The smell of it was sickening to me. I also knew it as a drug for petty criminals. Career criminals typically do not steal from their immediate families to support their drug addiction.

Crack was able to reach a larger population of users than many of its predecessors. The new addicts did not have the skills to hustle and obtain money to feed their addiction. They often support their habits by taking advantage of their family and friends. Prior to crack's inception, there were principals upheld even within the drug culture. Drug users did not typically do some things. Killing immediate family members were taboo. Usually, stealing occurred outside of the immediate family; it was perpetrated against other people. Many of the new addicts were not adept at the most advanced forms of hustling and street games. They began to steal from their families, jobs, and friends. Normally, the addict possessed a measure of reserve in their thievery.

I don't know what possessed Buck to try crack. He had seen the effects of the drug. With this drug, there was no room in his life for me. Buck had his own holes needing to be filled. He kept looking for answers in the drugs. This ultimately kept him revolving in and out of prison. While he was in prison, I had to be the head of the house. I was determined to be good at it and I eventually became comfortable in the role.

> *And shall not God avenge His own elect,*
> *which cry day and night unto Him, though*
> *He bear long with them?*
> **Luke 18: 7**

In the beginning, I was begging Buck to stop abusing drugs. Then, I began begging God to deliver him. Finally, I was no longer asking Him to deliver Buck, I was begging for permission to end the marriage. The last time I asked God about divorcing him, there was no answer. God was silent. I took this as permission to do it my way.

When I decided to end the marriage, the love was still there. I loved Buck and I knew that he loved me. Love just wasn't enough. I was his second love. His first love was the drugs. We needed something stronger than love if the marriage was going to survive. It seemed to me that we didn't have what it was going to take for the survival of our relationship.

> *And if a woman shall put away her husband,*

and be married to another, she committeth adultery. **Mark 10:12**

Frustrated with his lifestyle, I walked away from the man I loved. I decided to let God have him because I just couldn't handle him anymore. When I told him I had filed the papers for the divorce, I don't think he believed me. He tried to talk to me, but my mind was made up. Knowing he would not sign the divorce papers, I filed for divorce by publication.

But godliness with contentment is great gain.
1 Timothy 6:6

After my divorce, I was content to remain single. During this time, God began to deal with me about submission in marriage. It was a hard message and I knew that I needed help in this area. It was also during this time that I learned a lot about sharing financial resources. Both lessons were hard for me to digest. Nevertheless, I was resolved should I ever remarry, I would try it this way.

The Second Time Around

As for God, His way is perfect: the word of the LORD is tried: He is a buckler to all those that trust in Him.
Psalm 18:30

A few months before Jim's death, I reconsidered my relationship with Buck. There were several things that influenced my decision. There is a saying that you know the poison that you have, but you don't know the one you may get, or in other words, pick your poison. I had years of experience choosing the wrong partners. Thoughts of dating were scary to me. I had no desire to remain single, but I was afraid of dating. When I thought about Buck, I decided that he loves me, unconditionally. At least, we call it love. It may be more accurate to say he wants me in his life at any cost. His perception of love has been clouded by his past.

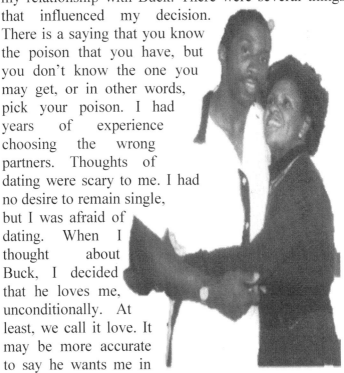

For all this I considered in my heart even to declare all this, that the righteous, and the

wise, and their works, are in the hand of God: no man knoweth either love or hatred by all that is before them. **Ecclesiastes 9:1**

Love is supposed to be unconditional. Even in marriage, it's often hard to love this way. There is often the expectation that we can change the person into what we want them to be.

Without knowing God, it's impossible to know, receive, or share real love. Without God, love is a selfish, self-seeking love. The expectations are often, "What can I gain from this relationship?" This is often unrealistic, especially when you have nothing to offer. In any relationship, there is a measure of giving and taking. It is seldom a 50-50 partnership. However, when the person who gives only 20% demands a right to 120 or 150%, there is a terrible imbalance. Chaos and confusion are inevitable. How can love, marriage, or any relationship survive under these conditions?

Husbands, love your wives, even as Christ also loved the church, and gave Himself for it; **Ephesians 5:25**

My expectations of love were distorted by years of reading romance novels and watching soap operas. For years, I have been waiting for the man who still believes in chivalry. He opens the door for you. He pulls the chair out for you. On the days when you work late, he prepares dinner or at least takes you out to eat. He prepares bubble baths and rubs my aching back and feet. He looks for opportunities to give. He's compassionate and understanding. He's honest and trustworthy. He's good looking and intelligent. He comforts me when I'm hurting. He's hard working and goal oriented. He's a man of prayer and commitment. He provides for his family. He shares my pain and my sorrows. He pushes me to achieve my dreams. He works to fulfill his own dreams. We have common dreams, goals, and objectives. He seeks what's best for me. He's committed and devoted to me. He leads by example. Most of all, he loves the Lord.

When I became a Christian, my expectations from my husband became more clouded. I actually thought that if my husband loved me the way the Bible said, our lives would be ideal. If a man loved you like that, wouldn't submitting be easy? If a man loved you like his own body, wouldn't he be considerate of your needs? I fell in love with the book of Ephesians, particularly the fifth chapter. I longed for the day when I could have a marriage like that.

Don't worry about anything; instead, pray about everything. Tell God what you need, and thank Him for all He has done. If you do this, you will experience God's peace, which is far more wonderful than the human mind can understand. His peace will guard your hearts and minds as you live in Christ Jesus.
Philippians 4:6-7 NLT

After Jim's death, I went to Buck for comfort. It was hard to hide the pain. It was hard to explain the place Jim held in my life. He had been a part of my life for so many years. Jim wasn't the man I had dreamed about for years. He was just Jim. I hoped Buck would understand what I couldn't explain. The pain I felt was hidden in my heart. There were only a few tears. It didn't feel right.

When Buck was released from prison, I picked him up. During the drive home, we stopped at a courthouse and were remarried. This ended a six-year separation and divorce. We rushed into the second marriage as quickly as we had rushed into the initial relationship. This was an act of desperation. I didn't want to flirt with the temptation of sin. In many ways, I married a stranger for the second time.

For if you just listen and don't obey, it is like looking at your face in a mirror but doing nothing to improve your appearance. You see yourself, walk away, and forget what you look like. But if you keep looking steadily into God's perfect law--the law that sets you free--and if you do what it says and don't forget what you heard, then God will bless you for doing it.
James 1: 23-25 NLT

It had been more than sixteen years since our first marriage. Yet, we were still strangers. It is difficult to know someone when they're unwilling to reveal their true self. When you don't know something, it is impossible to understand it. If you are afraid to look in the mirror and behold your true self, you will never become what you have the potential to become. This will also affect every relationship in our life. Relationships will suffer when honesty is absent. Our relationship with Christ suffers when we attempt to deceive the one who knows everything about us.

I met Buck at a time when my life was broken and shattered. Jim had hurt me and I wanted to move on with my life. It created a terrible paradox that lasted for too many years. I chose to ignore my feelings for Jim. It seemed easier than confronting them. More importantly, I was running from God. Without knowing myself, it was impossible to give myself to someone completely. How can you give what you don't possess?

Charity suffereth long, and is kind; charity envieth not; charity vaunteth not itself, is not puffed up, Doth not behave itself unseemly, seeketh not her own, is not easily provoked, thinketh no evil; Rejoiceth not in iniquity, but rejoiceth in the truth; Beareth all things, believeth all things, hopeth all things, endureth all things. Charity never faileth: but whether there be prophecies, they shall fail; whether there be tongues, they shall cease; whether there be knowledge, it shall vanish away. **1 Corinthians 13:4-8**

There were so many issues clouding my perceptions of reality. I went into the relationship with Buck without knowing myself. Buck had his own issues. The night we met, brokenness met brokenness. Trouble embraced trouble. Confusion stirred confusion. Chaos invoked chaos. We complimented each other's negativity. When we married, hopelessness joined hopelessness in matrimony.

Therefore if any man be in Christ, he is a new creature: old things are passed away; behold, all things are become new. **2 Corinthians 5:17**

When I committed my life back to God, I became someone Buck didn't know. I became someone that I didn't know. With an earnest declaration, I vowed to give God more than I had given the devil. This was an enormous commitment. My salvation became the priority. Later, my spiritual, emotional, intellectual, and social growth became priorities. Before, we had our sins and our crimes in common. This had been the primary purpose for our relationship, breeding sin. With the sin fellowship gone, what did we have in common?

While I was focusing on my spiritual and personal growth, Buck continued to battle with drugs and crime. As I struggled to build a new name and reputation, he wasted more years inside the prison system. The last separation was more than six years. It was during this time that my life made the most drastic changes.

> *Take a lesson from the ants, you lazybones.*
> *Learn from their ways and be wise! Even*
> *though they have no prince, governor, or*
> *ruler to make them work, they labor hard all*
> *summer, gathering food for the winter. But*
> *you, lazybones, how long will you sleep?*
> *When will you wake up? I want you to learn*
> *this lesson: A little extra sleep, a little more*
> *slumber, a little folding of the hands to rest*
> *and poverty will pounce on you like a bandit;*
> *scarcity will attack you like an armed robber.*
> **Proverbs 6:6-11 NLT**

While I was moving into the future, Buck was trapped in a time warp. The prison system can ensnare your mind, and spirit, in addition to your body. It is a system that can cripple you for the rest of your life. It can rob you of any ability to reason logically or make the minutest decisions. You are told what to eat, what to wear, where to sleep, when to bathe, when to sleep, when to eat, how much to spend, when to spend it, where to go when you leave.

And that is why I am suffering here in prison. But I am not ashamed of it, for I know the one in whom I trust, and I am sure that He is able to guard what I have entrusted to Him until the day of His return.
2 Timothy 1:12 NLT

I have my own horror stories from the times my freedom was taken away. Most of my life, I have been able to choose what I eat. Prison or jailhouse food leaves much to be desired. I vowed never to eat anything that I didn't like. The first time I spent more than a day in jail, my diet consisted of sodas, candy, and rolls. By the time that I was released, my digestive system was out of control.

My prison sentence also left its mark. When I was released, a woman removing any piece of clothing in my presence repulsed me. Additionally, I didn't want anyone sleeping in the room with me. Eleven months surrounded by women had been too much for me.

As I was advancing my formal education, my dreams were clouded by fear. It was hard to believe anyone would hire an ex-convict. Although I have worked for numerous agencies since that time, a small doubt that someday my past would return to haunt me has lingered. In spite of this, I have to risk failure. If I never risk failing, I have already failed.

While in prison, the government provides you with the basic necessities of life, shelter, food, clothing, and a measure of safety. All people have a need to belong. Prison affords the inmate the opportunity to become a member of an exclusive clique.

A prison is a place where an enormous amount of time is wasted counting days and months until your release from prison. While incarcerated, you wish your days to pass quickly, moving closer to your release. Countless hours sleeping help to facilitate the illusion of time passing quickly.

After months or even years of being denied the privilege to make decisions, you are released without rehabilitation and instructed to become a productive member of society. How do you awaken your brain from sleep? How do you recapture the time that you have lost? How do you find a place of comfort in a world that has moved on without you? For many offenders, the answer is you don't. Often times, they return to what is familiar, prison.

Look straight ahead, and fix your eyes on what lies before you. Mark out a straight path for your feet; then stick to the path and stay safe. Don't get sidetracked.
Proverbs 4:25-27 NLT

After years of seeking immediate gratification (quick fixes, easy money, shortcuts, and taking advantage of others), it is difficult for ex-offenders to assimilate into the working world (mainstream society) where limited resources often reduce or eliminate conspicuous consumption. Long work hours are often very foreign concepts to those accustomed to sleeping in while others are performing traditional jobs. Limited professional and academic skills may hinder the inmate's ability to obtain a job making a living wage.

A lack of motivation and limited self-confidence can further cripple the inmate's ability to assimilate into society. They may be more comfortable relying on the previous tricks and games that they have attempted unsuccessfully to master for numerous years, rather than risking failure in society. They may choose subconsciously to return to an environment where they commanded respect on a limited basis among their peers, other criminals.

> *But when it pleased God, who separated me from my mother's womb, and called me by His grace, To reveal His Son in me, that I might preach Him among the heathen; immediately I conferred not with flesh and blood: Neither went I up to Jerusalem to them which were apostles before me; but I went into Arabia, and returned again unto Damascus. Then after three years, I went up to Jerusalem to see Peter, and abode with him fifteen days.*
> **Galatians 1:15-18**

In every situation, we have choices. People or a system can imprison our physical bodies. However, we can choose to keep our minds free. Freedom comes from God. He gives us freedom that no one can take away.

Just as Paul was in the wilderness for three years being taught of the Holy Spirit, prison can be a wilderness experience. It can be a time of deep fellowship, in addition to personal and spiritual growth. Prison can provide a time of consecration. It is a place where 'jail house religion' can become a 'lifetime relationship.' Religion is merely tradition, not relationship. No one has to settle for religion or tradition. God wants a relationship with us. He wants to spend quality time with us. Prison can become the place to establish this relationship with Him.

> *Seek ye first the kingdom of God, and His righteousness; and all these things shall be added unto you.* **Matthew 6:33**

My aunt and uncle loved to play the numbers (the bug). For more than forty years, my aunt called her numbers in every day at 10:00 a.m. In the latter years of her life, her memory began to fail. She forgot family and friends. However, she never forgot some things. She never forgot her husband of more than sixty years. She never forgot to boil the water to wash the dishes. Most of all, she never forgot that at 10:00 a.m. she was supposed to call her numbers in. She remembered the things that she had practiced consistently.

> *My people are destroyed for lack of knowledge: because thou hast rejected knowledge, I will also reject thee, that thou shalt be no priest to Me: seeing thou hast forgotten the law of thy God, I will also forget thy children.* **Hosea 4:6**

During incarceration, many inmates condition their physical bodies to perfection. The same efforts should be applied to conditioning the mind and spirit. The mind and spirit need regular exercise. How can you exercise your mind and spirit?

We exercise our minds by acquiring positive knowledge. Opportunities for learning are all around us. Even in prison, there are opportunities to learn. Reading is an opportunity to exercise the mind. Television can become exercise equipment. It can be used for more than entertainment. It provides the opportunity to stay knowledgeable about an ever-changing world.

We exercise our spirits by spending time reading the Word of God. As we read, we should pray for wisdom, knowledge, and understanding. It is important to surround ourselves with other Christians who have a desire to please God. It is vital to apply what we learn.

Be ye not unequally yoked together with unbelievers: for what fellowship hath righteousness with unrighteousness? and what communion hath light with darkness? **2 Corinthians 6:14**

When Buck was released from prison, it was impossible for us to pick up where we left off. That place didn't exist anymore. My life had changed so much. In many ways, his life had stood still. I tried to mold him into the man that I had dreamed about for so many years, the man of my dreams, and the man of my fantasies.

Buck had his own ideas. He saw nothing wrong with himself. As I pushed, he pulled. It was frustrating to both of us. I wasn't satisfied with anything less than the man that lived in my dreams. He wasn't willing to put a lot of effort into changing. Moving forward in our relationship was going to require change. I wasn't going backward. If we continued the tug of war, we were going to move further apart. We were going to become more unequally yoked.

In order for our marriage to survive, some things would have to change. If we were going to work together for our future, these things would have to change quickly. There would have to be a drastic change. God would have to become the focus and foundation of our relationship. How could we blend such different lives without God as the equalizer?

Head to Head

For a husband is the head of his wife as
Christ is the head of His body, the church;
He gave His life to be her Savior.
Ephesians 5:23

My schedule is often hectic. After our second

marriage, there was no time for a honeymoon. My new life is demanding. Each day, I spend countless hours preparing for my ministry. In an effort to repair the mistakes of the past, I devoted my life to making amends for the pain that I had caused. If Buck was going to become a part of this life, he had to find his place quickly. He wasn't ready.

Buck was still trying to adjust to a world that had changed drastically during his incarceration. In many ways, life passed him by. In prison, all responsibility for his welfare had been left to the prison system. Within a few weeks, any dreams of a honeymoon were crushed and we were left with reality. Our lives had grown in different directions. The relationship was in trouble again.

Buck wanted to be the head of the house.

However, he had no experience in this area. On the other hand, I had lots of experience. For years, I had been a single parent. Even in marriage, I had been a single parent. During his battle with drugs, crime, and the prison system, I was the head of the house. Prison hadn't prepared him for this responsibility. My life experiences hadn't prepared me to relinquish control of the house. The desire to submit wasn't enough to make it happen. There would have to be a measure of trust before I could resign my role. Past experiences and broken trust said it was better for things to remain as they were.

> *Since everything around us is going to melt away, what holy, godly lives you should be living! You should look forward to that day and hurry it along.*
> **2 Peter 3:11-12 NLT**

When I went to prison, Buck was left to manage the house. Within days, things were out of control. His mother even advised me that I had made a mistake. We had also gone through periods where he had worked legally and attended church. Inevitably, because his mind had not been renewed, he continued with what I call stinking thinking. Stinking thinking is doing the same things you have done for years and expecting different results.

Previous attempts to get Buck involved in the household management had been unsuccessful. He was concerned about the finances coming into the house. However, he displayed no interest in what was going out of the house financially. This is not to say that he didn't contribute financially to the household.

For most of our relationship, Buck has contributed to the household when he wasn't in prison. There were also times that he made financial contributions to the household during his incarceration. He would find a way to prosper by illegal activities inside the prison. In spite of all of this, making sure there are enough finances to cover the household expenses has never been a priority. He trusts me to perform this task. To him, it seems logical that everything will be paid. Why shouldn't he make this assumption; everything has always been paid? He further assumes that I always have extra money that I have ready access to. He's not the only person who makes this assumption.

Live in harmony with each other. Don't try to act important, but enjoy the company of ordinary people. And don't think you know it all! **Romans 12:16**

Where was Buck supposed to learn the skills that he needed? There is no easy way to learn to be the religious and financial head of the family. Time and patience are required to acquire the necessary tools and skills to lead a family. In the past, he had never needed these tools. There were so many things that he needed to learn. Rather than risking seeming inept, he refused to acknowledge his need for help. This often resulted in him feeling as information was being kept from him in an effort to embarrass or humiliate him.

While in prison, an inmate is prevented from doing and learning things that are commonplace to those on the outside. Often, technology has advanced rapidly and those on the outside view it as common knowledge. Microwaves, DVDs, cellular phones, and even cable TV can be foreign to those not exposed to the latest advances. Furthering his education formally or informally was not a priority for him. I was ready to teach him if he was willing to learn.

Education is vital to my existence. I have made a commitment to learning or attempting to learn something new each day. When faced with something unfamiliar, it seldom intimidates me. I'll usually tackle the task with determination. If it beats me the first time, I learn from my mistakes. In the end, I usually master the task. Some of the things that I do best are things I struggled with in the past. By God's grace, I have limited skills in a variety of areas. These include sewing, auto mechanics, home repair, crocheting, cooking, catering, decorating, counseling, teaching, and facilitating workshops.

Now I beseech you, brethren, by the name of our Lord Jesus Christ, that ye all speak the same thing, and that there be no divisions among you; but that ye be perfectly joined together in the same mind and in the same judgment. **1 Corinthians 1:10**

Many of my skills are self-taught or learned. As I attempt to learn in my trial and error method, excessive hours are often lost. Because I learn *my way*, it can be difficult for me to learn the established method. Sometimes, it can be difficult to teach others my concepts. From an early age, this has been the way that I acquire knowledge. This can be intimidating for someone who does not learn in this manner. It can also appear that I have more knowledge of a subject than I actually have.

When I was in school, I was more advanced than some students in my classes were. Rather than waste my time, I often moved ahead of the teacher. Once I had mastered one assignment, I moved on to the next assignment or chapter in the book. Assignment may be the wrong word. In my rush to move ahead, I often completed lessons that were never assigned. Additionally, math was sometimes a problem. My methods of solving the problems were different than what the teacher instructed. Once I learned my method, it was often difficult to comprehend another method. Since many of my assignments were completed prematurely, my instructors understood the answers were not copied. Allowing for my unique learning style, they gave me credit for the final answers.

While I was working towards my bachelor's degree at Columbus College, computers were foreign to me. The secretary in the Health Sciences Department typed all of my papers for me. They were perfect and free of errors. When I began working on my graduate degree from Troy State University, I didn't have the same privilege.

One night, I turned in a typewritten paper that was full of my handwritten corrections. On my way home that night, I stopped by America's favorite store and purchased a computer. Although I had taken computer classes at Columbus College, my computer skills were minimal at best. Today, I have mastered computers. Now, I can operate most computer programs. I have also installed computer hardware and software.

During the last ten years, I have purchased

numerous computers. In the process of acquiring my computer skills, several computers suffered in the process. Technical support provided from the manufacturers was my best friend. At this point in my life, these telephone calls are limited. My skills may seem unobtainable to someone who has no computer skills. However, I am far from being classified as a computer expert or wizard.

Buck and I have very different approaches to learning. Because of my zeal in facing new challenges, many people rely on me for advice. When I don't have the information that I need, I won't deter until I get what is needed. When I was acquiring many of my skills, Buck was incarcerated. He never observed the time or efforts that prepared me for my current professions. He often underestimated the preparations and assumed there was an easy way to perform many tasks. This further strained our relationship.

It is better to dwell in a corner of the housetop, than with a brawling woman in a wide house. Proverbs 21:9

Because the bulk of the responsibility for my family has rested on me since I was sixteen years old, it is difficult to imagine that things could ever be any other way. This does not just include those in my household. There are others who rely on me for emergency support in some manner. This creates a situation where I feel that I am constantly giving out of myself. There are times when I feel emotionally bankrupt, because I'm not receiving what I am giving out. This creates a dangerous imbalance, which eventually has a volcanic effect. When I feel that I have had enough, I blow up. Usually, I get everybody at once.

Where there is no vision, the people perish:
but he that keepeth the law, happy is he.
Proverbs 29:18

Another side effect of having been in this role for so long is that I have the vision for my family. Once I know the direction that we need to move in, I commit to that direction. I also commit to the actions that will be necessary for us to get there. Failure is never considered as an option. Even if it becomes necessary for me to carry the primary responsibility or all of the responsibility for my family, I will not deter from the challenge. In the process, I often wear myself out both physically and emotionally. If something goes undone for an extended period of time, it can be almost guaranteed that I'll fix it or destroy it trying.

When Earline was in college, she developed a saying. Whenever I fixed a crisis for her, this was her response.

Laughingly, she would say, "What do you need with a man, when you have a Mama?"

She said this because many of the things that I did are usually delegated as male rather than female responsibilities. For me, it doesn't matter. Even if the tire needed changing and I was dressed in a new expensive silk outfit, my first response would be to change the tire myself. If roadside assistance arrives quickly, that's good. However, I'm not prone to wait idly for their arrival. This response comes from years of having to do it myself.

Often, I prefer to complete task myself with the

aid of my family rather than employing outside assistance. This can be frustrating to my family. I am willing to sacrifice countless hours to fulfill the vision. Sometimes, they are not quite as committed. Normally, they would prefer that I employ a professional, whereas, I may choose to make the repairs myself.

Buck wanted to be treated as the head of the household. However, this could only be delegated authority. He was accustomed to my fixing everything that went wrong, too. Financially, economically, spiritually, morally, and emotionally, he wanted me to maintain the role. He wanted to be a figurehead delegating responsibility. If he was going to be the head of the house, it would have to be in words and deeds.

Buck and I are different in almost every area. There are differences in parenting style. I am a stricter disciplinarian than he is. My expectations are high for my children. In my efforts to help them become all that they can be, I help with the task. My goals and expectations for myself have to be higher than the ones I have for them. Before Buck returned home from prison, this time, he was laid back and easy going, often attempting to befriend the children. The positive side of this is that he was easy for children to talk to. The negative impact of this was that it made it easy for the children to manipulate him. This would inevitably lead to a conflict between us.

So many things about him were different than I remembered. He had always doted on our granddaughter, LaToya. He was even different her. However, she was still able to manipulate him, causing problem for both of them.

When Buck came home, this time, he had

changed. He was overly sensitive in many areas. Conversation with him was difficult. He was quick to point out flaws in others. This created another conflict. I am *the defender of black sheep*. I'll quickly take the side of the underdog. As Buck pointed out flaws in others, I looked more closely at his faults. Because of my years of experience in this area, with each attack, he came up on the losing end.

> *But my life is worth nothing unless I use it for doing the work assigned me by the Lord Jesus -- the work of telling others the Good News about God's wonderful kindness and love.* **Acts 20:24 NLT**

There were other problems. During his absence, my efforts had been concentrated on learning to submit to God. His efforts had been concentrated on submitting to another authority, the penal system. The penal system has the ability to crush the spirit of any man or woman.

> *The Spirit of the Lord GOD is upon me; because the LORD hath anointed me to preach good tidings unto the meek; he hath sent me to bind up the brokenhearted, to proclaim liberty to the captives, and the opening of the prison to them that are bound; To proclaim the acceptable year of the LORD, and the day of vengeance of our God; to comfort all that mourn; To appoint unto them that mourn in Zion, to give unto them beauty for ashes, the oil of joy for mourning, the garment of praise for the spirit of heaviness; that they might be called trees of*

> ***righteousness, the planting of the LORD,***
> ***that he might be glorified.***
> **Isaiah 61:1-3**

In my efforts to be obedient to God, I had stepped out on faith. I had given up working a traditional job. My sole purpose in life had become to do the will of God. In the process, I had learned to cast my personal reservations and fears of embarrassments aside. Some things had not been easy but through it all, God's grace was sustaining me. My blind obedience to God often meant inconveniencing myself.

Buck needed things in his life that my relationship with God wouldn't allow. He needed security and structure. These were things he learned in prison and brought home with him. My prison stay had taught me something else. Prison taught me the importance of freedom. I didn't need man to govern or correct my actions. God has provided my instructions in His word. If I obey God, structure and discipline are things that I can apply to my own life.

> ***Jesus saith unto him, I am the way, the truth,***
> ***and the life: no man cometh unto the Father,***
> ***but by Me.*** **John 14:6**

Salvation and holiness aren't inherited. They don't rub off because you engage in an intimate relationship with someone who has obtained salvation by grace. It's not something that you are born with. You can't force someone to choose what God has allowed them the free will to reject. Association or immolation doesn't provide salvation. It's not a learned behavior. It is the free gift of God. He has provided the directions to unwrap this gift in His Word. There are no shortcuts or quick fixes. Even the most adept thief can't steal his way into the kingdom of God.

During our separation, several spirits had gained a stronghold on Buck's life. They were his friends and he wasn't ready to identify them as enemies. These spirits weren't bashful and they wanted to be acknowledged. They were bold and deceitful. They reared their heads at every opportunity. They were attracted to other immoral spirits.

Everyone will know that the LORD does not need weapons to rescue His people. It is His battle, not ours.
1 Samuel 17:47 NLT

Before long, romance gave way to complacency and idleness. In spite of the strain on my marriage, I continued with my hectic schedule. As I worked countless hours, he attempted to maintain the schedule that he had become accustomed to in prison. As I worked, he often slept.

I often denied myself sleep to accomplish the things that had to be completed. My body was tired. My mind was tired. My spirit was tired. I felt myself growing weaker. I felt a massive attack from the devil headed my direction. However, the attack had already begun and my weapons weren't ready.

Love Hurts

*Fools have no interest in understanding; they
only want to air their own opinions.*
Proverbs 18:2 NLT

In the beginning, the attacks against me were subtle. On more than one occasion as I was traveling, a car pulled into my path. By God's grace, my life was spared. Buck and I weren't communicating. There were so many things that he needed to learn. He resented the teacher, me. There were things he hadn't been taught. There were other skills that were unnecessary skills for street life. They were unnecessary in prison.

Because I seldom retreat in the face of a new challenge, I can be demanding. I often ponder or undertake several different tasks at one time. By God's grace, I have acquired a variety of skills. To acquire these skills, I have to risk failure. To an untrained eye, I may appear skilled in an area that is unfamiliar to me. This can be irritating or intimidating to someone who is uncomfortable or reluctant to undertake new experiences.

While Buck was in prison, we made plans for our future. He would attend classes at a local technical college a few hours a week. He would develop the necessary skills to work beside me in business. When he wasn't in school, he would work with me in the office or in the field.

Before he was released, I set things in order for his return. It was a perfect plan. There were a couple of problems. It was my plan. It wasn't his plan. It wasn't our plan.

> *God did not send His Son into the world to*
> *condemn it, but to save it.*
> **John 3:17 NLT**

He had no desire to attend the school. Additionally, we were still unequally yoked. I had assumed that Buck had surrendered his life to God during this incarceration. He was so adamant about not going back to prison. Once again, I had gotten my signals crossed. I was still a sucker for a love story with a fairytale ending. I was still waiting for my knight in shining armor to sweep me off my feet. We were still going to live happily ever after.

> *But the fruit of the Spirit is love, joy, peace,*
> *longsuffering, gentleness, goodness, faith,*
> **Galatians 5:22**

When reality hit me in the face, I didn't enjoy the picture. After a few weeks, my fantasy was gone. It was back to trying to make Buck surrender all to God. This seemed a simple task to me. As I pushed for the man that I had been dreaming of, I became more dissatisfied with the one that I had married. I looked for books to address the issues that I identified. I found none.

> *Pride ends in humiliation, while humility*
> *brings honor.* **Proverbs 29:23 NLT**

Marriage is work. It's hard work. There are days when it's like chocolate covered cherries. In spite of its sweetness, there are days when it's more like a hot kosher pickle. As I attempted to help Buck acquire new skills, our diet moved more towards pickles and cayenne peppers.

One day, as we were working in the office, Buck crossed an invisible barrier. For years, I had supported the household. During his numerous absences, I was the head of the house. Each time he returned home, I assured that all of his material comforts were provided for.

Because that, when they knew God, they glorified Him not as God, neither were thankful; but became vain in their imaginations, and their foolish heart was darkened. **Romans 1:21**

When he returned home from prison for the final time, rather than being thankful for all the things that had been provided for him, he complained about the things he didn't have. He had squandered these things, during his addiction. Although I had nothing to do with the things that led to his incarceration, I attempted to replace the things he no longer possessed. In many ways, his complaining made me feel used. However, I kept these thoughts to myself. Buck blew my fuse with one statement. He started a war that neither of us knew how to stop.

He stated with assurance, "You take me for granted!"

But love ye your enemies, and do good, and lend, hoping for nothing again; and your reward shall be great, and ye shall be the children of the Highest: for He is kind unto the unthankful and to the evil. **Luke 6:35**

His assertion was a joke. He had no idea how

many things I did for him. He was about to learn. I was determined to teach him. The battle lines were drawn. I was going on strike. It was time for him to learn responsibility. If he was going to become responsible for the household, he would first need to become responsible for himself. It was time for him to find another job. How can you control what you don't own or possess? How can you reap where you haven't sown? How can you lead where you haven't prepared to go?

His statement drew the battle line in our relationship. It made me think about being taken for granted. When I considered our relationship, I was sure that I was the one who had been taken for granted. That was about to stop. Enough was enough!

Supporting him during his incarcerations should have been enough for him. He didn't even appreciate that generosity. Now, I had offered him a place in the life that I had made without him. He assumed that he had a right to that place.

I hearkened and heard, but they spake not aright: no man repented him of his wickedness, saying, What have I done? every one turned to his course, as the horse rusheth into the battle. **Jeremiah 8:6**

When I stopped catering to his needs, he had no idea what had gone wrong. He eventually apologized or he tried.

With sadness in his eyes, he said, "Sister, I'm sorry for whatever I have done to turn you against me."

There was no need for the apology. I hadn't turned against him. However, I had come to realize I had contributed to the problems that he was having. For years, I had been Miss Fixit. Whenever he stumbled, I had been there to catch him. No matter what he did, I had tried to correct the problem.

That I may know Him, and the power of His resurrection, and the fellowship of His sufferings, being made conformable unto His death. **Philippians 3:10**

Each time he was arrested, I would rush to make his bond, run to secure a lawyer, and try to minimize his punishment.

Whenever he was serving time, I tried to make him comfortable in prison. I did his time with him. I made regular weekly visits to the prisons, wrote countless letters to him and the parole board, sent money orders, and packages. Rather than allowing God to have free course in Buck's life, I kept begging God to lighten the punishment. I was unwilling to let him endure his just punishment, which may have God's way of drawing him nearer to Him. He needed to spend time with God. He needed to learn how to trust Him. Each time he returned home, I tried to make his transition back into society seamless. I made sure that he had a new wardrobe.

For do I now persuade men, or God? or do I seek to please men? for if I yet pleased men, I should not be the servant of Christ. **Galatians 1:10**

During his final incarceration, I withheld some of the amenities I usually provided. Nevertheless, I knew that upon his release, he would have difficulty finding a job making legal livable wage. I rushed in to fix that problem. I had crippled him as much as the prison system. It was time to remove the crutches. If he would attempt to walk on his own, I was willing to help him. However, I wasn't willing to carry him or drag him.

> ### *For my love they are my adversaries: but I give myself unto prayer.* Psalm 109:4

Buck didn't like tough love. While I firmly stood my ground, he resisted making these changes. His rebellion turned to hurt and pain. I couldn't see the pain. All I saw was laziness and excuses.

Our lives would never be the same. Never again would he take me for granted. Even if he did, he would find the crutch was no longer there. I was willing to hand him the directions, but I wouldn't bait the hook and I wouldn't swing the rod. It was time for him to learn to fish. If he were willing to do the catching, I would do the cooking. Was it too late for him to learn? If he didn't attempt to learn, was our marriage doomed?

The Second Knock

When thou passest through the waters, I will be with thee; and through the rivers, they shall not overflow thee: when thou walkest through the fire, thou shalt not be burned; neither shall the flame kindle upon thee.
Isaiah 43:2

After several weeks, Buck found a job. Rather than alleviating some of the problems that we were experiencing, it created new problems. The job required him to work a rotating schedule. This often conflicted with my schedule. The salary was another issue. The job was more than thirty miles away. We only had one car.

Approximately, a week after he began working, we had another problem. In fact, it was another major crisis. Television can distort our reality of many things. How we see things enacted on television can lead us to make the false assumption that reality occurs in this manner.

Fire had almost destroyed my life once. By God's grace, I had survived. It seemed impossible that fire would strike at my life again, but it came calling again.

My mother and I had spent the day together. As we ended our day, she asked me if I wanted her to spend the night at my house. Buck was scheduled to work through the night. I preferred having someone at home with me. Herman had recently returned from college. However, his hours were unpredictable.

Normally, my morning begins around 8:00 a.m. On the morning of July 6, 2004, I was awakened at approximately 5:30 a.m. This was unusual for me.

During the night, I hadn't heard Herman come home. He had an appointment in a couple of hours. After walking to his room, I discovered him asleep. He's a sound sleeper, but I needed to know what time he wanted to rise. After I woke him, he told me and went back to sleep. Since I was awake, I decided to walk through the house. My nephew had come home with Herman. He was sleeping in the den. I walked down the hall to the room where my mother was sleeping in my granddaughter, LaToya's room. Concerned that I would fall back off to sleep, I asked my mother to awaken Herman in about thirty minutes. She typically begins her day earlier than I do.

God is our refuge and strength, a very present help in trouble. Psalm 46:1

When I returned to my room, I noticed my pocketbook sitting at the end of the bed. Herman had moved my pocketbook from the den because he had company. It wasn't long before I was asleep again. After about fifteen minutes, I was awakened again. Mama was shaking me.

With alarm, she said, "Get up! I think that I smell something burning. I thought somebody had left the iron on, but it wasn't plugged up. After you woke me up, I decided to get up so I wouldn't oversleep."

As I walked down the hall, my nephew was coming from the den.

Still half asleep, he said, "Somebody is burning something."

We began to look through the house for the source of the smell. It was just a mild smell. When I opened the washroom door, I noticed a laundry basket sitting near the hot water heater. The basket was starting to melt. A small flame was extending from the water heater. It appeared that it would be easy to extinguish. I ran to the kitchen, a few feet away. After quickly locating a cup, I began to fill it with water. Before the 32-oz. cup was half-full, smoke had begun to fill the house.

Mama had already gotten Herman up. Quickly, I attempted to call 911. They didn't answer on the first ring and I didn't have time to wait. I ran to my room for my pocketbook. By the time, I walked back up the hall, I couldn't see the living room or the front door. Herman was directing me to the door. After we made it outside, I went to my neighbor's house to call for help. I also called my sister. She lived three or four blocks away. Next, I called Earline. It was about 6:15 a.m.

As I was trying to get help, Herman was trying to find a way to get water into the house. Smoke was starting to seep from the windows of the house. We still didn't hear the fire trucks coming. I have a newfound appreciation for pulling over when a fire truck is approaching.

We didn't have time to dress before running from the house. Although we were all dressed inappropriately, my mother's appearance concerned me. My mother was wearing a slip and a T-shirt.

I prayed, "Lord, please don't let the television cameras come."

We hadn't died in the fire, but Mama would have died from embarrassment if she had been seen on the evening news in a slip. My sister arrived and the fire trucks still weren't there. As she parked her car, Mama met her.

With nervous anxiety, my sister asked, "What happened?"

The drama queen, my mother, responded, "We could have all died. It's just the grace of God that we are still..."

My sister interrupted my mother, "No you couldn't have. God wouldn't do that to me. He knows I couldn't have taken that."

As we stood and watched the house burning, one of the neighbors brought us chairs so that we could be seated. When the firemen finally arrived, I was sitting there, helplessly watching years of memories being destroyed. At the time, I told myself the things that I needed to hear to remain calm. The fire was going to be confined to the washroom. It was just stuff. Everything in the house was replaceable. We're still living; that's all that matters.

> *It is a good thing to receive wealth from God and the good health to enjoy it. To enjoy your work and accept your lot in life -- that is indeed a gift from God.*
> **Ecclesiastes 5:19 NLT**

As we waited, the frame of the front door began to separate. The firefighters went into the house three times before the fire was quenched. After the third time, one of the firefighters walked out of the house and stood next to the den's window. He removed his mask and lit a cigarette. Two thoughts came to my mind. The first one was, "Hasn't he inhaled enough smoke?" The second thought was, "How rude. This is a non-smoking house." Ironically, smoke was still coming from the house.

As I was watching him, the spokesperson for the unit walked up to me. I saw her approaching, but I wasn't really focused on her.

She spoke calmly, "I need to speak with the owner of the house."

My answer was just as calm; "I'm Charlotte Johnson."

She replied, "I need to prepare you to go into the house. You'll need to get your insurance policy. If you can tell me where to find you a pair of shoes, I'll bring them out to you."

For the first time, I noticed my bare feet. I told her where to find my shoes. A few minutes later, she emerged from the house without the shoes. She said that she was unable to find any. I thought this was strange, but I didn't comment. Someone loaned me a pair of tennis shoes. She continued her attempts to prepare me to enter the house. My family had gathered around me.

She instructed, "No one else is allowed in the house."

As we walked into the living room, she supported my arm. In spite of her warnings, my family followed us into the house. My mother was worried about her favorite Bible. It had been in the den and she was determined to recover it. She headed straight for the den. Although it was near the heart of the fire, her Bible was unharmed.

Stay away from the love of money; be satisfied with what you have. For God has

said, "I will never fail you. I will never forsake you." **Hebrews 13:5 NLT**

Nothing could have prepared me for the devastation. The ceilings in the living room, dining room, kitchen, and hall were collapsing. Wet insulation covered the furniture. Lamps, porcelain, crystal, and brass were scattered throughout the house. The television in the den had melted into the entertainment center. Clothes and shoes were thrown everywhere. A mirror hanging at the end of the hall was folded in half. The house had a horrible smell. The ceiling was continuing to fall. I kept telling myself, "It's only stuff." I needed to stay calm.

Following my retrieval of the insurance policy, I was instructed to leave the house. After I made the preliminary telephone calls to the insurance company, we just sat on the porch waiting. Waiting for what? I don't know, just waiting.

There was no way to call Buck to let him know what had happened. After working a twelve-hour shift, he arrived home. We were still sitting on the porch. He was surprised to see us all sitting outdoors.

Confused, he asked, "Why are you sitting on the porch?"

I pointed him towards the house. He made his way past the people sitting on the porch and walked into the house. After a few minutes, he returned looking more confused. We explained briefly, what had happened. Subsequently, he returned to the house. When we heard a loud crash inside the house, we tried to account for everyone's whereabouts. Buck was the only person missing. We went inside looking for him. The ceiling was still falling. Buck was in the bed sleep.

We had to awaken him.

Later that afternoon, the insurance company called. Arrangements were made for temporary shelter. We checked into a hotel. This was supposed to be an ordinary day. It was anything but ordinary.

Ephesians 5:22-33

Wives, submit yourselves unto your own husbands, as unto the Lord. For the husband is the head of the wife, even as Christ is the head of the church: and He is the saviour of the body. Therefore as the church is subject unto Christ, so let the wives be to their own husbands in everything. Husbands, love your wives, even as Christ also loved the church, and gave Himself for it; That He might sanctify and cleanse it with the washing of water by the word, That He might present it to Himself a glorious church, not having spot, or wrinkle, or any such thing; but that it should be holy and without blemish. So ought men to love their wives as their own bodies. He that loveth his wife loveth himself. For no man ever yet hated his own flesh; but nourisheth and cherisheth it, even as the Lord the church: For we are members of His body, of his flesh, and of His bones. For this cause shall a man leave his father and mother, and shall be joined unto his wife, and they two shall be one flesh. This is a great mystery: but I speak concerning Christ and the church. Nevertheless let every one of you in particular so love his wife even as himself; and the wife see that she reverence her husband.

Selene

There is a path before each person that
seems right, but it ends in death.
Proverbs 16:25 NLT

In the late 1970s, Jim arrived in Columbus. He brought with him a young son and daughter by a previous marriage and Cathy, one of his women. My daughter and his children were very close in age. Earline, my daughter was four. Lil' Jim was three and Selene was five. Selene was Jim's oldest daughter. In many ways, she became my daughter.

How can a young person stay pure? By
obeying Your word and following its rules.
Psalm 119:9 NLT

From the beginning, Selene would tell me the things that her father didn't want me to know. He tried to stop her and this upset me. He never mastered this task. If he made the mistake of letting her see it, she told me.

From the beginning, it seems the odds were against Selene's survival. She saw too much. She endured too much. From the time of her birth, she was exposed to a life that was unsavory. Many behaviors that are considered anti-social were a routine part of her upbringing.

The old sinful nature loves to do evil, which
is just opposite from what the Holy Spirit
wants. **Galatians 5:17**

From an early age, she learned not to trust anyone. She learned to guard her heart against hurt. In many ways, her behavior often seemed not only selfish but also heartless. If she found herself getting too close to someone, it scared her. If you got too close to her, she would find a way to hurt you. Stealing from you usually provided the means to hurt you. If you were too kind to her, she would immediately look for an opportunity to hurt you first.

My mother and I had talked for several years about opening a restaurant; however, we had never done anything to move towards that direction. Mr. Stone owned the Tally-Ho Grill. My friend, Pat worked for him at another restaurant. One day, Pat called me.

She said, "Mr. Stone wanted to know if you are interested in running the Tally-Ho."

I responded, "I'm really not interested in working."

She responded, "I don't think he wants you to work for him. Just come and talk to him."

I didn't really know Mr. Stone and the only thing that he knew about me was that Pat respected my opinions. Curious, I went to talk to Mr. Stone. The conversation lasted almost five minutes.

He said simply, "Do you think you could handle the Tall-Ho?"

I responded just as simply, "Yes sir!"

He told me to make a list of all the items that I would need to open the restaurant and he asked me to come back the next day. Still unsure what he had in mind, I showed up the next day with my list. He took me to the grocery store and purchased everything that I had on my list and gave me the keys to the restaurant.

His only instructions were for me to come see him after I had completed my first week.

When we opened the restaurant, Selene and Earline came to work for me. At the age of fourteen, Selene was already living with her boyfriend and his parents. Each morning, we picked her up at their house in route to the restaurant.

We opened the doors of the restaurant without even a dollar to go into the cash register. The menu consisted of a large variety of soul food, including chitterlings, ribs, pig feet, pig ears, black-eyed peas, collard greens, macaroni and cheese, and homemade sweet potato pies, etc. We served breakfast and lunch. My mother would assist with cooking before she went to work each morning. On her lunch hour and again when she finished her regular job with the Housing Authority, she would return to help me with cooking and serving the food.

The first Saturday evening after we closed, I was scheduled to meet with Mr. Stone. During our meeting, I was to update him on my week. The Business had been good from the first day that we opened the restaurant. Financially, we were off to a good start.

Men do not despise a thief if he steal to
satisfy his soul when he is hungry;
Proverbs 6:30

That Saturday when we arrived at the restaurant, I put the money into the cash register. The remainder of the money was hidden in my purse. A few minutes later, Selene went to the restroom. She remained there for some time. When she emerged, she was barely able to walk. She sat down at one of the booths. I continued preparing the food. When the first customer paid for his food, I got a major surprise. The cash register was empty! The money was also missing from my purse. We were opening the business for a second time that week with no money in the cash register.

After the customer left, I searched Earline and Selene. The money wasn't in their pockets or purses. A short time later, Selene said she needed to leave because she wasn't feeling well. She said she was going to get someone to give her a ride home. As she walked across the street, I watched from the door of the Tally-Ho. She was barely able to stand up straight. I choked back my tears and my anger.

There was a strange twist to Selene's antics. She wanted you to know when she had bitten you. When I got the opportunity, I called Chuck. Selene had been to his house. When I told him what had happened, he wasn't surprised.

He said, "She showed me the money. She said that you had paid her. I knew something was wrong. I wondered why you had given her so much money."

I wasn't Selene's first victim or her last. It was, however, the only time that she bit me.

He that dwelleth in the secret place of the most High shall abide under the shadow of the Almighty. I will say of the LORD, He is my refuge and my fortress: my God; in Him will I trust. **Psalm 91:1-2**

At the end of the day, I went to meet with Mr. Stone. He wanted to know if I had purchased the additional supplies that were needed for the following week and paid my help. Only after these items were taken care of, he wanted 25% of what remained. I didn't tell him that during the week someone (someone close to my heart) working for me had also stolen all of my money from the cash register and my purse. By God's grace, I had enough money to pay him.

> *And let us not be weary in well doing: for in*
> *due season we shall reap if we faint not.*
> **Galatians 6:9**

Mr. Stone was an accountant. Included in his 25% was the cost of him completing the taxes for the business. He informed me that when I was comfortable with the restaurant, I could just give him $125 a month for the use of the equipment and assume responsibility for the other expenses. The other expenses were less than $200 a month. A month later, I took over the restaurant completely.

Selene and I never discussed what had happened that day. She was already experimenting with drugs. What happened that day never affected our relationship. Even in my pain, I understood what she had done. Selene had a practice of hurting you before you could hurt her.

As Selene grew older, she added new skills. These skills eventually caused her legal problems. When she was incarcerated the last time, she wrote me a letter apologizing for the things she had done to me. What had hurt me most were the things that she had done to herself.

Before Selene was imprisoned, she began to have health problems. My efforts to get her to monitor her health were met with resistance. She would call me only if she was scared. Before she was released from prison, her health deteriorated.

The day after her release, I took her for a medical examination. Her skin and eyes were both discolored. Some other things were obviously going awry with her health. We were there for several hours. Several people examined Selene. She insisted that I stay by her side. In her eyes, there was a look of fear. Several times, a tear swelled in the corner of her eye. She held them back. I held back my own tears.

Between the examinations, we visited with one of my friends who worked in the building. She had been aware of Selene's condition from its onset. Selene joked about the things going on with her health. The condition wasn't funny, but her jokes were. We laughed with her.

When your faith is tested, your endurance has a chance to grow. **James 1:3 NLT**

After Selene's last examination was completed, a second appointment was scheduled for the next day. She needed tests that are more extensive. When I dropped her off that afternoon, she asked me to pick her up the next morning. Before morning arrived, Selene had left the city. Actually, she moved to another city.

Before Selene's release on parole, she had been assigned to a halfway house. A halfway house is designed to assist you in making the transition from prison. You're not free, but you are allowed a measure of freedom. During your stay there, you are allowed to obtain employment outside the prison system. During her time at the halfway house, Selene met friends. She decided to visit these friends.

Several weeks went by before Selene called me. She assured me that she was monitoring her health. She was trying to build a life there and had obtained employment. At the time of her call, she reported that she was still drug-free. It wasn't long before she moved again. She moved to a distant state.

Thou wilt shew me the path of life: in Thy presence is fulness of joy; at Thy right hand there are pleasures for evermore.
Psalm 16:11

A few months after Jim died, Earline had a disturbing conversation with Selene. She told Earline that she was dying. Additionally, she said that she needed to see me. Immediately, Earline conveyed the information to me.

There was less than five minutes difference between the end of Selene's conversation with Earline and the beginning of her conversation with me. When I called Selene, she made light of the conversation with Earline. I wanted to see her. Selene told me that she was going to a party. She was planning to attend church on the following day. She promised to call me after she returned from church. The call never came and I was unable to contact her.

A few days after my house caught on fire, Earline received a call about Selene. After the telephone call was completed, Earline contacted me to share the information.

Obviously upset, she said, "Mama, I just received a telephone call. Selene is in the hospital in intensive care. It doesn't look good."

When I called the hospital, I asked for Selene's room. She wasn't in intensive care. In fact, she answered the telephone in her room.

Surprised to hear her voice, I asked, "What's going on?

In her usual whine, she responded, "I had a bad cough, but I'm better now. Are you coming to see me tomorrow?"

Confused by these very conflicting reports, I responded, "I don't know. My house caught on fire. I lost almost everything I own. Trying to get things straightened out has taken over my life. I'll call you."

Remember not the sins of my youth, nor my transgressions: according to Thy mercy remember Thou me for Thy goodness' sake, O LORD. Psalm 25:7

There was nothing unusual about Selene's voice. It often appeared that she reverted to a child during our conversations. Whenever she was scared or sick, this would happen. There wasn't much that scared Selene. At least, she didn't show the signs of fear. There were times when I believed she was scared. They weren't often.

Over the past few years, there had been several close calls with her health. She refused to let self-pity win. Although her lot in life had been rough, I never heard her say, "Why me? Why is this happening to me?"

It was several days before I attempted to call Selene again. When I called, she was no longer in the hospital. This wasn't unusual. She had been in and out of the hospital on numerous occasions. Each time after she was released, she returned to her normal routine. Because she hadn't called me, I assumed she had recovered and returned to the streets.

One Saturday morning, I met Earline and my granddaughter, LaToya for breakfast at a local restaurant. As we began to eat, Earline gave me the news that destroyed my appetite. As she was driving to the restaurant, she had received a telephone call.

Almost in one breath, she said, "Mama, Selene died."

The restaurant was crowded. This was not the place to give way to my emotions. There were so many questions to be asked. For most of them, I would find no answers. Why hadn't Selene told me how sick she was? Why hadn't she called me this time? Where had she been? She had always called me when she was scared, why not this time.

And He said unto me, My grace is sufficient for thee: for My strength is made perfect in weakness. Most gladly therefore will I rather glory in my infirmities, that the power of Christ may rest upon me. **2 Corinthians 12:**9

My heart was aching. It had been aching for some time. The ache was growing deeper. So many things had happened to me in such a short period of time. I couldn't handle this one. It would have to wait. With everything else going on, I didn't have time to grieve. My time was running short to complete the repairs to the house. I had already advised the insurance company of my plans to move back into the house. If I gave in to my emotions, we would never move home.

I placed this grief in the pile with the rest of the

things that I didn't want to deal with. However, I deceived myself. I believed I was being strong and resilient. I was multi-tasking. It appeared I was able to handle multiple traumas without crumbling under the pressure. I was focused and persistent.

Broken Walls

Every house has a builder, but God is the one
who made everything.
Hebrews 3:4 NLT

The walls of the house weren't the only walls that were damaged the day of the fire. As I began to seek help to rebuild the house, I made all the wrong choices. I wanted to be a financial blessing to family and friends. My efforts were rewarded with greed and treachery.

"Do not nurse hatred in your heart for any
of your relatives." Confront your neighbors
directly so you will not be held guilty for their
crimes. **Leviticus 19:17 NLT**

It became necessary for me to spend countless hours at the house. Actually, it was no longer a house; it was a shell. Initially, everyone in my family was willing to assist with repairing the house. My desire to complete the house was so strong that for months I worked from morning to late evening buying materials and laboring on the house. I was willing to give up all recreational activities including TV. My family worked along with me. After several weeks of working, they began to grow bored with the task. They began to rotate time assisting me with the repairs on the home.

Remodeling my house after the fire was not the first major project for the family; in the past, we have painted a home in one day and raked over a hundred bags of leaves in one night. My family typically complains, but later they agree to assist me. My tendency to push myself to the limit and Buck's desire to relax and enjoy life often compete.

Typically, I seldom ask others to do for me what I can do for myself. My husband takes the opposite approach. The problem with my doing things myself is that my physical strength often fails in the process. Although I was diagnosed with several disabilities after I was burned, I have chosen not to live my life catering to the conditions. In the absence of a volunteer to do simple chores that may be physically strenuous, I just do it. Later, I suffer the aches and pains for it.

Buck has a very different method of dealing with these inconveniences. If it is at all possible, he prefers not to get dirty. He would rather pay someone else to perform the task. In the absence of the funds, he will allow it to go undone. The flip side of this is that if I don't have the money, I'll attempt to fix it.

Buck prefers having recreational and relaxation time. My desire and drive are to work and support my family. I can't relax when my pockets are void of finances. Our competing or conflicting approaches became more prevalent after the fire. Sleep remained a priority for him. My priority was getting back into the house. He trusted me to handle this task. He was content to do what was convenient for him. I didn't have that option. The head of the house never has the option of convenience. The head of the house has to do whatever it takes to maintain the household.

My friends scorn me, but I pour out my tears to God. **Job 16:20 NLT**

As people sought to benefit financially from the tragedy that had befallen my family, it added to the weight of the pain. It hurt most that it came from those closest to me. If someone was going to take advantage of me, I preferred that it be a stranger, not those that I had been subsidizing for years and not those of the household of faith. When I could take no more, I cried out to God for someone to help me.

The day after I prayed, my mother was sitting on the porch of the house. A man pulled up in a truck. This stranger offered to help us. He was the answer to my prayer. He did what family and friends were unwilling to do; he gave me a fair price for a good job. He was also willing to work quickly to get me back into my home.

How precious is Your unfailing love, O God!
All humanity finds shelter in the shadow of
Your wings. **Psalm 36:7 NLT**

Being homeless was hard on me both physically and emotionally. An enormous amount of my time had to be committed to repairing the damage to the house. There were countless papers to be completed for the insurance company. They wanted to know what was in the house, where was it located, how many we had, how long did we have it, how much did it cost, and how much it would cost to replace it. They also wanted to know which items were gifts. As if this wasn't enough information, the mortgage company had their own set of questions and requirements.

It was difficult for me to sleep through the night. My sleep was constantly disturbed. Several times during the night, I walked through our temporary apartment checking on my family. For days after the fire, I smelled like barbecue. The smell of smoke was always with me. It was in every room of the house. Even after the walls were knocked out, I still smelled the smoke.

My marriage to Buck crumbled under the weight of the pressure that I was experiencing. In many ways, I felt he wasn't offering me enough support. He had his own set of complaints. Our arguments became more heated and more frequent. I was tired of the arguments and the lack of communication. Arguments don't facilitate communication. If there are any messages relayed during an argument, they always communicate the wrong message. I was ready for a reprieve.

How forcible are right words! but what doth your arguing reprove? **Job 6:25**

After a particularly intense argument, I asked him to move out of our temporary apartment. While he was in the bathroom, I removed his keys from his key ring. Buck had to unpack his car in order to pack his belongings. The car was being used to store part of the items that I was purchasing for the house. As he brought the items in, he sat them next to a chair in the living room.

After Buck left the apartment, I went on to church. As the offering was being taken up, I noticed my credit cards were missing. Immediately, I left the church and returned to the apartment. When a quick search failed to locate the missing cards, I canceled all my credit cards. Afterward I performed a more thorough search. This included turning over the chair near where my pocketbook had been sitting. This was the second time in three hours that I flipped the chair over.

> ***Thou therefore which teachest another,***
> ***teachest thou not thyself? thou that preachest***
> ***a man should not steal, dost thou steal?***
> **Romans 2:21**

On the previous evening, I had used one of the credit cards at a gas station. At the time, I was alone in the car. My pocketbook had remained locked in the car until we returned to the apartment. Herman was gone when we arrived at the apartment. He didn't come home that night. Earline, LaToya, and my mother followed me to the apartment that night. Buck was already there.

> ***Keep me from deliberate sins! Don't let them***
> ***control me. Then I will be free of guilt and***
> ***innocent of great sin.***
> **Psalm 19:13**

Earline was authorized to use my business bank account. Before going to church that morning, I couldn't find one of the shoes that I wanted to wear. In the process of looking for the shoe that morning, I had overturned this chair. When I returned from church looking for my credit cards, the chair was turned over for the second time. I had been the last person to leave the apartment that morning. Mama was at church. Earline and LaToya had also left the apartment. We were all going to meet at the house. We all returned to the apartment together that night.

After Buck left the apartment, he went to his

mother's home. When I called the house, I was told that he had gone to the grocery store.

I left this message for him, "Tell Buck that my charge cards are missing."

All day, I waited to hear from Buck. He never called. That night Earline, LaToya, my mother, and I arrived at the apartment together. Rather than sitting in my normal chair, I sat on the sofa adjacent to the chair. When LaToya sat down in the chair, I noticed something in a corner of sheet that was thrown across the chair. It was my cards stacked neatly together. I had turned over twice this same chair. As I held the cards in my hand, the telephone rang. To my surprise, it was Buck. I had given up on him calling.

In a very casual tone, he asked, "What was the message you left for me?"

Angrily, I responded, "I said my credit cards were missing."

Calmly, he said, "Where are they now?"

Without answering his question, I hung up the telephone. There was one thing that I was sure of; earlier in the day, the cards hadn't been in that chair.

My soul is also sore vexed: but Thou, O LORD, how long? Psalm 6:3

In order to reactivate my cards, I had to go into a branch of my local bank. I asked the customer service representative to verify the activity on my cards during the last forty-eight hours. Someone had attempted to use both my business and personal bank cards, approximately ten minutes after I blocked the cards. The attempted purchase amount was $11.46.

We who have fled to Him for refuge can take

new courage, for we can hold on to His
promise with confidence.
Hebrews 6:18-19

When I arrived at the apartment that night, I began making plans for the second divorce from Buck. We separated on a Sunday morning; on the following Thursday morning, I filed the divorce papers. The divorce petition had been downloaded from the Internet. The papers were filed in the clerk of Superior Court's office. The divorce cost me a little over a hundred dollars. It seemed a small price to pay for my freedom. At least, the divorce was supposed to make me free. Approximately thirty days later, the divorce was final. That is, I had the final decree in my hands. The judge's signature was in the appropriate place.

Familiar met Familiarity

Regard not them that have familiar spirits,
neither seek after wizards, to be defiled by
them: I am the LORD your God.
Leviticus 19:31

After our separation, one of the spirits that had a stronghold on Buck's life decided to show himself strong and mighty. He had denied his presence, but the spirit was no longer content to destroy him quietly. The spirit sought the aid of another familiar spirit to destroy him. The second spirit had been waiting for him for years. Although I had identified the spirit years before and warned him of the true intent of this spirit, he entertained it.

Don't be fooled by those who try to excuse
these sins, for the terrible anger of God
comes upon all those who disobey Him.
Don't participate in the things these people
do. For though your hearts were once full of
darkness, now you are full of light from the
Lord, and your behavior should show it!
Ephesians 5:6-8 NLT

There is blessedness in realizing our sinfulness. We can never obtain salvation by grace if we cover or excuse our sins. Light does not serve the same purpose as darkness. The person who covers their sins will never manifest light. Our behavior should reflect and bear witness to our confession of faith.

And Judah said unto Onan, Go in unto thy

*brother's wife, and marry her, and raise up
seed to thy brother. And Onan knew that the
seed should not be his; and it came to pass,
when he went in unto his brother's wife, that
he spilled it on the ground, lest that he
should give seed to his brother.*
Genesis 38:8-9

When he was at his weakest point, the spirit moved in for a full attack. He was flattered by the attention. Two familiar spirits united and attempted to justify their actions in the Word of God. Deceiving only themselves, they manifested the deeds of darkness and called them deeds of light.

*For the name of God is blasphemed among
the Gentiles through you, as it is written.*
Romans 2:24

Many people assume that those who call themselves by the name Christians or saints are representatives of Christ. Christian means "Christ-like." When those who profess the name of Christ manifest behaviors that are inconsistent with the nature of Christ, they cause sinners to blaspheme the name of God. By their very behavior, they suggest this is the way Christ would act in this situation.

*For there is no faithfulness in their mouth;
their inward part is very wickedness; their
throat is an open sepulcher; they flatter with
their tongue.* **Psalm 5:9**

I knew Sister Juanita when she was just Juanita. It had been more than twelve years since she visited our home with one of my in-laws. This was the first time that she met my husband. Indirectly, she began to flatter him with her words.

"Oh Charlotte, your husband is so good looking and handsome. He's so nice to you."

When I could take no more, I responded, "He's not all that."

Determined to drive her point home, she responded, "Why would you say that? He's so nice to you."

I repeated my previous statement. However attractive I found my husband, he didn't need a strange woman with flattering lips to reinforce it.

The next day, Buck went to visit his mother. Sister Juanita was there. Shortly after his arrival, I received a phone call. The voice on the other end of the telephone was familiar to me.

My mother-in-law stated with alarming force, "You better get over here! This woman is after your husband. She's over here telling him how good he looks."

My mother-in-law was never one to mince words. This was not the first time that she warned me about something inappropriate. It was not the first time she warned me about a woman. As in times past, I heeded this warning.

A naughty person, a wicked man, walketh with a froward mouth. He winketh with his eyes, he speaketh with his feet, he teacheth with his fingers; Frowardness is in his heart, he deviseth mischief continually; he soweth discord. **Proverbs 6: 12-14**

A short time later, Sister Juanita set her sights

on another family member. Under the pretense of witnessing to him, she began to write my brother-in-law. It didn't take long before romantic undertones began to develop. After the affair ended without a wedding ring, she moved on to the next family member. She found success here for a limited period. When the relationship became shaky, she began to write my brother-in-law again. This didn't work out for her.

Behold, therefore I will gather all thy lovers, with whom thou hast taken pleasure, and all them that thou hast loved, with all them that thou hast hated; I will even gather them round about against thee, and will discover thy nakedness unto them, that they may see all thy nakedness. **Ezekiel 16:37**

When my brother-in-law passed, Sister Juanita wanted to speak at his funeral. She told the immediate family of her unfailing love and devotion for him. I thought this was inappropriate. She was still married to his first cousin. The family bond between them had never been severed. They grew up together in the same community and enjoyed a close friendship as adults. In many ways, they were as close as any brothers were.

Sister Juanita was not legally separated from her husband. The couple was experiencing marriage problems, which was their typically cycle. When I made out the funeral program, I listed her as a cousin. I did not want her to humiliate herself and her husband further. The family did not need to be separated during this period of mourning by further conflict. Her husband was also at the funeral. The next time that I saw Sister Juanita, she was with her husband. They were attempting reconciliation. She thanked me for intervening during my brother-in-law's passing.

The reconciliation didn't last long. Sister Juanita began looking within the same family for a new victim. It was about this time that she learned Buck and I were separated. She rushed in to capture a new prey.

***With her much fair speech she caused him to yield, with the flattering of her lips she forced him.* Proverbs 7:21**

Sister Juanita was well adept at her game. She had years of practice perfecting her role in the church, a silly woman looking to entice men with flattering words. While doing this, she continued to confess salvation.

***Rend your heart and not your garments. Return to the LORD your God, for He is gracious and compassionate, slow to anger and abounding in love, and He relents from sending calamity* Joel 2:13 NIV**

In some religious sects, the emphasis is on modesty; however, a long skirt can serve more than one purpose. While I am an advocate for moderate apparel, true modesty comes from within. Modest women are not seducers or adulterers. True modesty shuns the very appearance of evil. Christian women should reflect the attributes of Christ. Their modest behavior should be obvious to any man. No modest woman should be identifiable as a loose woman. Modest women do not allow the passions of their flesh to flame their sinful desires.

But speak thou the things which become
sound doctrine: The aged women likewise,
that they be in behaviour as becometh
holiness, not false accusers, not given to
much wine, teachers of good things; That
they may teach the young women to be sober,
to love their husbands, to love their children,
To be discreet, chaste, keepers at home, good,
obedient to their own husbands, that the
word of God be not blasphemed.
Titus 2: 1, 3-5

What has happened to the teachings of the aged women? Do we wink at sin? Do we excuse sin for convenience sake? At what cost are we willing to ignore sin? How can darkness be excused as light? Is there still a difference between clean and unclean? Is there a difference between holy and unholy? The Bible clearly instructs us to make a distinction in all of these areas.

Ye adulterers and adulteresses, know ye not
that the friendship of the world is enmity with
God? whosoever therefore will be a friend of
the world is the enemy of God. **James 4:4**

Is the Word of God still true? Do we have a choice of which scriptures to obey? Are some sins greater than others are? Do we justify our sins by looking for fault in others? Does God give us instructions or directions that are contrary to His word? Are those who practice sinning at every opportunity members of the body of Christ? Is salvation a matter of convenience? At what point, do we become a partaker of another man's sin? Has the Word of God become of non-effect? For all of the questions that I have posed, the answers are fond in the Word of God. His word will never return void.

Abstain from all appearance of evil.
1 Thessalonians 5:22

Sister Juanita seduction started with an innocent ride to our church. After our separation, Buck's work schedule hindered him temporarily from attending church services. Reportedly, he needed support when he first returned to service. It may have been difficult for him to return to the church that we attended together. I have a lot of family at this church and he has none. However, I am not certain of the reason he required additional support. A relative offered to accompany him to church. Sister Juanita volunteered to drive them. Although Buck had transportation, he accepted the ride. I was absent from church the night they made their appearance.

So put away all falsehood and "tell your neighbor the truth" because we belong to each other. And "don't sin by letting anger gain control over you." Don't let the sun go down while you are still angry, for anger gives a mighty foothold to the Devil.
Ephesians 4: 25-27 NLT

Once she saw a crack in the door, she stuck her foot in it. Buck later told me, she made her intentions clear during a visit to see a sick family member. Because she married into this family, it was not unreasonable for her to visit this relative.

This is his account; "We were walking down the hall of the hospital. My nephew was walking beside me. She reached over and pinched my … Later, she asked me if I thought it was an accident. She asked me how it felt. I couldn't believe it."

But now I am writing you that you must not associate with anyone who calls himself a brother but is sexually immoral or greedy, an idolater or a slanderer, a drunkard or a swindler. With such a man do not even eat. **1 Corinthians 5:11 NIV**

After this incident, she invited him for a cozy dinner at her home. There were trips to her church and an introduction to her pastor. Ironically, as they attempted to justify their sins with scripture, the pastor's messages brought home a different message. Each time they attended the service together, the pastor spoke about adultery and fornication.

Shortly after my separation from Buck, I thought about Sister Juanita. I knew there was still an issue in her flesh for him. At the time, Buck was not my priority. He had offered little support during the fire. My family was homeless. At least, that's the way it felt. I was desperate to see my home restored. Some things would have to wait. I was sure Sister Juanita was on the prowl. Except for the grace of God, I wasn't expecting Buck to remain celibate after our divorce.

But evil men and seducers shall wax worse and worse, deceiving, and being deceived. **2 Timothy 3:13**

In some ways, I underestimated Buck; in other ways, I overestimated him. After living with Buck, I knew there was something lacking in his profession of faith. Except for the grace of God, the lust of the flesh and the pride of life can destroy even the most devout saint. Lust had been knocking at the door for some time. The pride of life was threatening to let it in. Being separated from me gave Buck the occasion to feed his lust, but not an excuse for the sin. Realizing that this might happen, I thought, he would be more discriminating in his choice. I never thought that he would settle for seconds or thirds from his brother and first cousin. Actually, I thought he had a measure of control over his flesh. I knew that Juanita would pursue him; however, I thought he was strong enough to withstand the temptation.

> *For the commandment is a lamp; and the law is light; and reproofs of instruction are the way of life: To keep thee from the evil woman, from the flattery of the tongue of a strange woman. Lust not after her beauty in thine heart; neither let her take thee with her eyelids. For by means of a whorish woman a man is brought to a piece of bread: and the adulteress will hunt for the precious life. Can a man take fire in his bosom, and his clothes not be burned? Can one go upon hot coals, and his feet not be burned? So he that goeth in to his neighbour's wife; whosoever toucheth her shall not be innocent.*
> **Proverbs 6:23-29**

It wasn't long before the secret was spread throughout the family. One of my nieces put it best. Although she didn't attend church regularly, she had learned something from a devout Christian woman. She shared this with several other family members and me.

This is the way the unconfessed saint described the confessed saint, "Whenever she sees someone acting all fast. She says, 'I smell a wh...'

I agree; I smell a wh..., a church wh...."

Buck later told me that he heard Juanita's son use a similar term to describe his mother. There is no polite or delicate way to talk about sin. Sin is an abomination to the Lord and stinks in His nostrils. When we attempt to soften, camouflage, or make excuses for sin we become partakers in that sin and bring damnation upon ourselves. The Bible is clear, woe unto those that sin and teach others to sin. God does not leave us in our sin; instead, He provides a way for us to be redeemed. He sits high and looks low. He desires to save the liar, the hypocrite, the church whore, the adulterer, the fornicator, murderer, and yes, even the wife who has thrown away her husband. Without faith, it is impossible to please God. He is able to repair what has been torn and to make what is dirty clean.

During a brief break in my schedule, I became concerned for one of my in-laws, but I didn't want to contact her. It might appear that I was seeking information about Buck. Additionally, I was so busy. After thoughts of her lingered for several days, I decided to put my personal feelings aside. After several unsuccessful attempts to reach her, I called another family member. She was distant but anxious to speak to me.

After a few minutes of formal conversation, she asked bluntly, "Do you want your husband or have you just thrown him away? There is someone hot on his trail."

And because iniquity shall abound, the love

of many shall wax cold. **Matthew 24:12**

It wasn't necessary for her to provide further information. I filled in the blanks for her.

She pleaded, "Help me get this woman out of my family! I don't understand the fascination with this family."

I assured her, "He may sleep with her, but he won't marry her. He still loves me. He's hurt and he needs to be saved."

From my experience, I know that fools who
turn from God may be successful for the
moment, but then comes sudden disaster.
Job 5:3 NLT

For several days, I pondered her words. "Did I want him?"

Truthfully, I wasn't sure. Sister Juanita was going to bring him down if I didn't intervene. My pride was at stake. In many ways, I felt like a fool for even considering taking him back. On the flip side, Juanita would feel that she had won some well sought after prize if I didn't put an end to it. After all, she had wanted my husband from the first time that she met him. When I thought about them both having a form of godliness (fakeness), I thought they deserved each other. He would never be able to trust her around any male member of his family. She would never be able to trust him around silly women. There were other things that they had in common. Maybe they did deserve each other.

Why was he going backward rather than moving forward with his life? If he stayed in the relationship guilt and shame was going to send him back to the streets and back to prison.

> *Even if he wrongs you seven times a day and each time turns again and asks forgiveness, forgive him."* **Luke 17:4 NLT**

In forgiving an offender, do we ever truly forget the offense? After we forgive the snake that has bitten us, do we embrace the snake? Do we embrace the snake if the snake claims to be a brother or sister in the Lord? Do we embrace them if the opportunity to continue the offense has ceased? Since I had initiated the divorce, did that make Buck fair game for my professed sister in the Lord? If so, is it appropriate date because you are unhappily married? Is it acceptable to divide a family by pursuing one incestuous relationship after another within the family? After divorce, is at acceptable to look for a new mate within the former spouse's family? If the answer is yes, are adultery and fornication ever appropriate? Are adultery and fornication still considered sins by the Christian church? At what point does God sanction a woman pursuing a man for any purpose?

After serious contemplation, I consulted my immediate family and a very close friend. Nevertheless, I knew that the ultimate decision rested on my shoulders. In the end, I needed to obey God rather than man.

> *Be not deceived; God is not mocked: for whatsoever a man soweth, that shall he also reap.* **Galatians 6:7**

One morning, I had a vision of seeing Buck with Juanita. They were walking into our church. My response was horrible. I told her that she could have him. This wasn't a sarcastic comment, but a serious one. I proceeded to tell her what it would take to keep him. In the process, I told her all of his favorite things, the food that he liked, the hairstyle he liked, and so the list went. I told her how to pretend to be me. It was definitely a spirit talking to me. However, I knew that it wasn't from God. That wasn't the way to handle it. Even in this situation, I needed to extend grace.

Therefore if thou bring thy gift to the altar, and there rememberest that thy brother hath ought against thee; Leave there thy gift before the altar, and go thy way; first be reconciled to thy brother, and then come and offer thy gift. **Matthew 5:23-24**

Buck had wronged his cousin and brought shame to his family and the name of the body of Christ. This guilt would be enough to consume him. In a moment of weakness, his flesh had overtaken his conscience and done severe damage to his mortal soul.

But she that liveth in pleasure is dead while she liveth. And these things give in charge, that they may be blameless. But if any provide not for his own, and specially for those of his own house, he hath denied the faith, and is worse than an infidel. **1 Timothy 5:6-8**

Buck's only hope of breaking free from the bondage of the sin that had ensnared him for so long was to surrender completely to the Lord. He was involved with someone who had confessed salvation and sanctification for years. In the midst of their continuous open sin, they professed that they were drawing closer to God.

Having a form of godliness, but denying the power thereof: from such turn away. For of this sort are they which creep into houses, and lead captive silly women laden with sins, led away with divers lusts, Ever learning, and never able to come to the knowledge of the truth. Now as Jannes and Jambres withstood Moses, so do these also resist the truth: men of corrupt minds, reprobate concerning the faith. But they shall proceed no further: for their folly shall be manifest unto all men, as theirs also was. 2 **Timothy 3:5-9**

One day, I decided that I wanted to talk to Buck. Since our separation, we had only exchanged a few civil words. The divorce had been final for approximately two weeks. Since we were attending the same church, I thought it was important for us to establish a more comfortable relationship. I tried calling him several times at his mother's house. He wasn't there. I knew where to locate him. The old Charlotte began to rise up. It had been a long time since I had acted so spitefully. In the beginning, I wasn't angry; however, I wanted him to know his sin had been exposed.

Since God chose you to be the holy people whom He loves, you must clothe yourselves with tenderhearted mercy, kindness, humility, gentleness, and patience. You must make allowance for each other's faults and forgive

> *the person who offends you. Remember, the
> Lord forgave you, so you must forgive others.
> And the most important piece of clothing you
> must wear is love. Love is what binds us all
> together in perfect harmony.*
> **Colossians 3:12-14 NLT**

It didn't take much to secure her telephone number. She answered the telephone when I called.

Holding back my laughter, I greeted her politely, "Hey Juanita. How are you doing?"

Puzzled, she responded "Blessed! Who is this?"

Eagerly, I responded, "This is Charlotte Johnson."

Shocked, she answered, "Charlotte what do you want?"

Mischievously, I retorted, "I want to speak to my husband!"

Confused, she shot back, "I didn't know he was your husband."

Firmly, I asserted, "He's been my husband for more than twenty years."

> *I know, LORD, that a person's life is not his
> own. No one is able to plan his own course.
> So correct me, LORD, but please be gentle.
> Do not correct me in anger, for I would die.*
> **Jeremiah 10:23-24 NLT**

By the time Buck took the telephone, I was really getting agitated. The tone of his response escalated my anger. My pride kindled with jealousy told me how to respond; however, instead of driving to her house, I chose to call my sister-in-law. We talked for hours. When we released the telephone, the sun was getting ready to rise. I didn't tell her all the thoughts of vengeance that were churning in my mind. When the time the conversation ended, I had made my decision. I wasn't giving my husband away.

Although there were still a lot of problems, I had worked hard to bring him this far. During our previous separations, Buck had always returned to his first love, drugs. This time, he had found a different medication. This one was just as addictive as heroin, cocaine, and crack. It was also just as deadly.

The Third Time Around

And she said unto him, How canst thou say, I
love thee, when thine heart is not with me?
thou hast mocked me these three times...
Judges 16:15

After the house was completed, something was missing. More than anything else, it was my peace of mind. For more than three months, the house had been filled with continuous noise. The sound of hammers, nails, drills, saws, and craftsmen had been almost nonstop. Now that the house was completed, the noise ceased. On numerous days, I was left alone. I was left alone with all the things that I had delayed dealing with. My pain and solitude threatened to consume me.

Listen to my voice in the morning, LORD.
Each morning I bring my requests to You
and wait expectantly. **Psalm 5:3**

When I began to grieve for Selene, it brought home the other deaths that I had failed to acknowledge. When I began to think about Selene, Reba, and Jim, depression overtook me. My body was so tired that I was easy prey. My efforts to shake it off seemed futile. When I was at my weakest point, I laid in bed hoping that answers would overtake me. They didn't come easy. Sleep wouldn't come.

It was obvious that I didn't want to be alone. It was time to deal with my marriage. This was the second time that I had divorced Buck without God's approval. Now, it was time to deal with my actions.

> *"Beware of false prophets who come*
> *disguised as harmless sheep, but are really*
> *wolves that will tear you apart.*
> **Matthew 7:15 NLT**

In spite of numerous warnings, I had rushed into the divorce. Juanita was the last person that I wanted Buck involved with in a relationship. For a long time, I had known that she was a wolf in sheep's clothing. As a member of the family, I liked his cousin. I had watched her husband struggling with his relationship with God for a number of years; however, I knew God's grace was still resting upon his life.

> *The LORD doesn't make decisions the way*
> *you do! People judge by outward appearance,*
> *but the LORD looks at a person's thoughts*
> *and intentions.*
> **1 Samuel 16:7 NLT**

My thoughts were torn. It seemed easy to throw Buck to the wolves. He deserved it. No one had forced him into the relationship. He could have chosen to resist the temptations of his flesh. God's grace said, "No, that's not the way."

> *For in many things we offend all. If any man*
> *offend not in word, the same is a perfect*
> *man, and able also to bridle the whole body.*
> **James 3:2**

There were too many people being hurt by what had happened. In the midst of this situation, three people needed immediate salvation, Buck, Juanita, and Juanita's husband. There were also others that needed salvation. They had been affected by what they had observed. This gave credence to the excuse that the church is full of hypocrites. Nevertheless, this is not an excuse for rejecting Jesus Christ, who is the marker for identifying a hypocrite.

> *God is Spirit, so those who worship Him must worship in spirit and in truth.*
> **John 4:24 NLT**

One night, I fell out of bed onto my knees. It wasn't that I got down on my knees. I literally rolled out of the bed onto the floor. I began to cry out to God in a way that I hadn't prayed in months. In the process, I cried for Reba. I cried for Jim. I cried for my broken marriage. I cried for Buck's salvation. Mostly, I cried for my darling Selene. Why did she leave me without a goodbye?

> *And shall not God avenge His own elect, which cry day and night unto Him, though He bear long with them?* **Luke 18:7**

When I arose from my knees, my strength had returned. God had given me what I needed, His grace. For breakfast, lunch, and dinner, my meat became His Word. In His Word, I found the comfort and reassurance that I needed.

> *But I say unto you, That whosoever shall put away his wife, saving for the cause of fornication, causeth her to commit adultery: and whosoever shall marry her that is divorced committeth adultery.* **Matthew 5:32**

With all the boldness that God has given me, I told Buck that the divorce was not according to God's will. While the Bible makes allowance for divorce,

divorce is never a mandatory solution. Infidelity was not the reason or excuse for the divorce. Buck tried to avoid talking to me or seeing me. This told me that he didn't trust his feelings for me. When he tried to avoid talking to me, I continued to speak the Word.

Be ye angry, and sin not: let not the sun go down upon your wrath: Ephesians 4:26

Wrath can be like a hot pot of coffee or a simmering pot of beef stew. It's dangerous to let it brew too long. As coffee continues to brew, it becomes stronger. Eventually, it is no longer palpable. As a stew continues to simmer, it becomes thicker. If the stew isn't watched carefully, it may even stick to the pot. Wrath has the potential to stick and become resentment.

A man's pride shall bring him low: but honour shall uphold the humble in spirit. Proverbs 29:23

Whenever partners have incompatible methods of resolving conflict, the issues may never truly be resolved. Pride can hinder any relationship. Wrath can brew to the point of destroying a relationship or family. When either party in a relationship has obvious difficulty accepting or acknowledging faults or mistakes, a crisis looms on the horizon. When apologies are slow to come, wrath continues to brew.

Rather than apologizing, some partners find alternate ways to resolve conflicts; however, these techniques may lead to an avoidance of the resolutions. One partner may attempt to resolve conflicts with the purchase of gifts. If the partner that receives the gift does not accept this as a resolution, it's a wasted gift.

Whenever a conflict occurs in my life, I have a

tendency to analyze them. Often, I over analyze them. In doing this, I am seeking to avoid repeating the problem. Buck has a very different way or method for resolving conflicts between us. After a period of missing the more positive interactions between us, he simply reverts back to the happier times. He often prefers not to discuss the conflict. Rather than risk another conflict, he will move to a comfortable place in the past and attempt to pull me with him. Temporarily, I may indulge him in the folly; however, since the conflict has not been resolved, it inevitably returns.

What shall we say then? Shall we continue in sin, that grace may abound? **Romans 6:1**

After I decided to restore our marriage relationship, I engaged in active campaign to break Buck's resolve to remain angry with me. He wasn't really angry with me. It was more that he placed a number of safeguards in place to teach me a lesson. Shortly after our separation, he informed his parole officer that our separation would be temporary.

Because of the multitude of the whoredoms of the wellfavoured harlot, the mistress of witchcrafts, that selleth nations through her whoredoms, and families through her witchcrafts. Behold, I am against thee, saith the Lord of hosts; and I will discover thy skirts upon thy face, and I will shew the nations thy nakedness, and the kingdoms thy shame. **Nahum 3:4-5**

Buck was acting totally out of character. He was uncomfortable talking to me. Whenever he spoke to me, he was sure to keep a safe physical distance from me. Sister Juanita had actively pursued a relationship with Buck. This included cooking for him. Actually, in some ways, it started with cooking for him. She was also pushing to finalize her own divorce quickly. A family member informed me, Sister Juanita was planning a quick wedding. This was without Buck's knowledge. I wondered how far she had gone in her plot. Were there other things in her pot that he had no knowledge of? When the saints began to pray, everything that she had cooked up came to naught.

Thou wilt keep him in perfect peace, whose mind is stayed on Thee: because he trusteth in Thee. **Isaiah 26:3**

When Buck made the mistake of letting his guard down temporarily, I reminded him of what I meant to him. He continued to resist repairing the mess that we had made. He made one declaration and attempted to stand on it.

He repeated continuously, "I have peace. God's not going against my peace."

Dear brothers and sisters, be quick to listen, slow to speak, and slow to get angry. Your anger can never make things right in God's sight. **James 1:19-20 NLT**

One day, I met Buck at his mother's house. He said that he wanted to dissolve things between us. We went into his bedroom to talk. He sat down on the bed and motioned for me to sit in a chair nearby. It was a difficult conversation. As he continued to proclaim his declaration of peace, I continued to quote scriptures. The conversation seemed to be going in circles, and then he said the wrong thing to me.

In a very cold tone, he said, "Tell it to the next …"

Before he finished the sentence, I jumped out of the chair and across the bed. This wasn't a planned attack. I caught him off guard and knocked him down. He was so shocked that he forgot to be angry. Before he could brace his response, he started laughing. Then, I kissed him. Afterward I had one question for him.

Knowingly I asked, "Did you see stars?"

With a smirk, he responded, "What do you think?"

After this initial contact, I assumed it was decided; he was coming home. He continued to take a hard line with me; however, I knew his resolve had been broken.

A few days later, I spoke to him over the telephone. As we completed our first civil conversation in months, we made plans to spend the next day together. It was hard to imagine things were turning around so fast. Originally, I expected another argument. The conversation had started with guarded formalities. In the middle of the conversation, he changed his conversation to one of endearment.

I will therefore that men pray every where, lifting up holy hands, without wrath and doubting. 1 Timothy 2:8

Our first day together was a day of continuous prayer. Buck initiated the prayers. He had never taken this initiative before. In spite of his relationship with Sister Juanita, he convinced me that he had learned to pray. It was something that I had pushed for before our separation. We made one promise after another. This would be different. That would be different. We would pray together each day. We would study our Bibles together. We wouldn't go to bed angry. And so the list continued.

> *For there shall arise false Christs, and false prophets, and shall shew great signs and wonders; insomuch that if it were possible, they shall deceive the very elect.*
> **Matthew 24:24**

When Juanita was unable to reach Buck by telephone, she knew immediately that he was with me. She bombarded my mother-in-law with ceaseless telephone calls. The telephone at his job saw no rest. We were told that she made one continuous statement.

With the boldness of a real saint, she proclaimed, "The devil is a lie!"

Juanita is right about one thing; the devil was and still is a lie. There are other things that she needs to know about him. He's a deceiver of men. His tactics are so cunning that he would fool the very elect if it was possible. It's not possible!

> *Ye are of your father the devil, and the lusts of your father ye will do. He was a murderer from the beginning, and abode not in the truth, because there is no truth in him. When he speaketh a lie, he speaketh of his own: for he is a liar, and the father of it.* **John 8:44**

On our second day together, we were remarried. This was hard for some people to accept. It was particularly hard for Juanita to accept. She drove to Columbus with her daughter supposedly to confront me. At least, I was told that her daughter wanted to see me. Juanita also gave my sister-in-law a message for my husband.

She threatened, "If he ever brings her to my church, I'll show out so bad. I'll embarrass him in front of everybody. I'll tell everybody that he is a hypocrite."

He that rejecteth Me, and receiveth not My words, hath one that judgeth him: the word that I have spoken, the same shall judge him in the last day. **John 12:48**

The true church is the body of Christ. Although we worship in physical buildings, no building is a church unless Christ dwells there. Juanita is not the pastor of this particular church. I think it would also be appropriate to say that based on her actions, she is not a member of the body of Christ.

Therefore, anyone who becomes as humble as this little child is the greatest in the Kingdom of Heaven. **Matthew 18:4 NLT**

Although I would like to say that Juanita realized the folly of her sinful ways and decided to turn from them, this has not been the case. I would like to say that I was the last person that she told how fine and good looking their husband was; yet, this continues to be her calling card. I would love to say that at last she has found the true meaning of salvation and established a relationship with Jesus Christ. Yet, she has remained a silly woman under the disguise of false modesty. The long skirts are still there. They are probably three sizes too small. She still has no boundaries and is enmeshed with my family.

Except for the grace of God, Juanita will bite

the next man in our family who is not aware of Satan's devices. My prayer remains that one-day, Juanita and those like her will repent and turn from their wickedness. I also pray for the poor souls who have been victims of a Sister Juanita.

By His Grace

Behold now, Thy servant hath found grace in Thy sight, and Thou hast magnified Thy mercy, which Thou hast shewed unto me in saving my life; and I cannot escape to the mountain, lest some evil take me, and I die: **Genesis 19:19**

Grace is God's loving, active presence in the world. Grace is usually defined as unmerited favor. Another way to express this is to contrast it with mercy. Mercy is God withholding what we deserve; grace is God giving us what we don't deserve. Grace is the free favor of God by which He has in Christ provided the way for our salvation. He has enabled us to embrace Christ.

If a soul sin, and commit a trespass against the LORD, and lie unto his neighbour in that which was delivered him to keep, or in fellowship, or in a thing taken away by violence, or hath deceived his neighbour; Or have found that which was lost, and lieth concerning it, and sweareth falsely; in any of all these that a man doeth, sinning therein: **Leviticus 6:2-3**

After about two weeks, the prayers turned to a long grace said over breakfast. The study time never materialized. Before long, he went back to an extensive sleep schedule. I went back to my computers. Soon after, it was marriage as usual.

Wise people treasure knowledge, but the

babbling of a fool invites trouble.
Proverbs 10:14 NLT

"I need this. I want this. I think this. I don't have. I deserve. We deserve. I can't. I'm doing the best I can do."

Inevitably, these answers came back.

"Where's your gratitude? It doesn't matter what you think; what does the Bible say? Why do you deserve? Why do we deserve? It's time to learn! You do what you can; I do what I have to."

Sometimes it praises our Lord and Father, and sometimes it breaks out into curses against those who have been made in the image of God. And so blessing and cursing come pouring out of the same mouth. Surely, my brothers and sisters, this is not right!
James 3:9-10 NLT

The arguments became more frequent, but they never changed. There was no family prayer. Communication became frustrating and tedious again. Then along came a little fudging or *a little white lie*. This went undetected. Then, there came a little deceit. The trust had never been reestablished. Deceitfulness has the potential to destroy any possibility of trust.

Our marriage had failed more than once. As in times past, we made promises and resolutions that this time would be different. It was only by God's grace that we found ourselves together again. We had said that this time, we were going to do it God's way. This promise was soon forgotten. When we neglected to pray together, we failed to acknowledge God. We were inviting adversity into our marriage again. When we fail to look to Him for answers, it is impossible for us to do it His way.

> *And now, brethren, I commend you to God, and to the word of His grace, which is able to build you up, and to give you an inheritance among all them which are sanctified.*
> **Acts 20:32**

Whenever, we attempt to do it our way, rather than His way, we are destined for trouble. God is always waiting for us to ask for His help and instruction. We both knew that we needed help. What keeps us repeating the mistakes of the past, when the answer is within our reach? We have numerous Bibles in our home and cars. In fact, the Word surrounds us. We even attend church regularly. Shouldn't Christians find solutions to their problems in the Word of God?

> *Now therefore, I pray thee if I have found grace in Thy sight, shew me now Thy way, that I may know Thee, that I may find grace in Thy sight: and consider that this nation is Thy people.* **Exodus 33:13**

Grace can be found all around us, among us, and within us. God constantly touches our lives, attempting to reach us through other people, places, events, and the material things we encounter every day. He loves us in spite of ourselves. He hates our sins.

> *For by grace you have been saved through faith, and that not of yourselves; it is the gift of God; not as a result of works, that no one should boast* **Ephesians 2:8-9 NLT**

There is nothing we can do to earn God's favor.

We are unable to please Him enough to be given His blessings. We certainly could never pay for our own sins and be saved. Grace in the form of love gives. It gives and demands nothing in return. God's grace is sufficient to save the most wretched sinner and the most troubled marriage.

Grace is a God given advantage and benefit. Without Christ, there is no mercy, love or grace. There is only hopelessness, wrath, judgment, and condemnation.

But where sin abounded, grace did much more abound. **Romans 5:20**

God's grace cannot be earned in any way. It is a

free gift. There is no way to merit grace. Grace is receiving what we don't deserve. In fact if God gave us what we deserve, we would be miserable and lost. God's grace must be received and accepted.

The believing spouse will discover that the continuous problems that arise from being married to an unsaved spouse will teach them to rely on and trust God more. Alternately if the believing spouse does not rely on God's grace to weather these trials, bitterness and resentment may develop. The believing spouse will not have the wisdom or the strength in himself to continue in the face of the seemingly insurmountable difficulties being faced. In spite of that, God has provided a wonderful solution to all of our problems.

All of our frustrations and problems can be poured out to God in prayer. With the confident knowledge that our God is still in charge, His grace will allow us to face all the challenges of tomorrow.

> *And he said if now I have found grace in Thy sight, O Lord, let my Lord, I pray Thee, go among us; for it is a stiffnecked people; and pardon our iniquity and our sin, and take us for Thine inheritance.*
> **Exodus 34:9**

The task that faces the saved spouse of an unsaved partner who is extremely upsetting to live with can become overwhelming. No individual in their own strength can overcome some of the difficulties that can arise in marriage. Only God's grace can sustain the marriage through these stressful situations.

Mr. & Mrs. Johnson

Inconvenient Convenience

"Don't store up treasures here on earth, where they can be eaten by moths and get rusty, and where thieves break in and steal. Store your treasures in heaven, where they will never become moth-eaten or rusty and where they will be safe from thieves. Wherever your treasure is, there your heart and thoughts will also be."
Matthew 6:19-21 NLT

God has a purpose and plan for marriage. While many desire a spouse or mate, there are various reasons for this desire. Some individuals hope to find completeness by uniting with another person. Some people marry for social, financial or material gain. Others marry for companionship or to avoid loneliness. Still, others marry to quench the fires burning in their flesh. This is not meant to be an exhaustive list of reasons for the commitment.

Be not deceived: evil communications corrupt good manners. **1 Corinthians 15:33**

When communication breaks down or ceases to exist, the injured parties may take refuge. They may find shelter in the wrong places or with the wrong people. When they decide the marriage is hopeless and there are no reasonable solutions to their differences, they may become roommates for convenience sake. Various reasons may contribute to their decision to remain married or to divorce.

For God is not a God of disorder but of

***peace.* 1 Corinthians 14:33 NLT**

Things are in danger of remaining out of order whenever God's will is not the primary consideration in any relationship. This is even more crucial in marriage. Any argument ends when we look into the word of God for honest answers and are willing to obey the instructions or corrections found therein.

God is our refuge and strength, a very present help in trouble. Therefore will not we fear, though the earth be removed, and though the mountains be carried into the midst of the sea; though the waters thereof roar and be troubled, though the mountains shake with the swelling thereof. **Psalm 46:1-3**

It is crucial in any household for the spouses to submit wholeheartedly to God. When this doesn't occur, God's order for the home is violated. God desires that the husband is the spiritual and economic head of the house. The woman is to be his helper or assistant. She is to assist him in maintaining the order of the house. In order for the husband to establish and retain order, he must maintain a consistent channel of communication with the Lord.

You will keep on guiding me with Your counsel, leading me to a glorious destiny.
Psalm 73:24 NLT

The spouse who has submitted their life to God will find difficulty submitting to a spouse who has not submitted to God. In an effort to please God, they will continue to try. In spite of their best efforts, when decisions or actions are contrary to God's will, conflict will be inevitable. God has a resolution for any conflict. It's found in His Word.

> *Hatred stirs up quarrels, but love covers all offenses.* **Proverbs 10:12 NLT**

In any disagreement or difference of opinions, it is vital to good communication to remain agreeable to an amicable resolution. When the parties are more interested in winning the conflict than reaching a positive resolution, healthy communication does not occur. Indeed, sometimes the communication is deadly. Hidden messages are often communicated. Sometimes, the message is "I intend to express my opinion, even when it's illogical to me."

> *Most important of all, continue to show deep love for each other, for love covers a multitude of sins.* **1 Peter 4:8 NLT**

When communication and actions move to a *tit-for-tat* mode, someone will always lose. The loser will generally be the person who brings the least to the relationship financially. In the end, both partners lose.

The person with the most financial resources has the ability to impose an economic embargo. The person with the least resources must be willing to give in other areas. An economic and relational imbalance occurs when there is a constant giving from one party. If the other party becomes accustomed to receiving without having to give, they may assume they are entitled to receive. The giver in the relationship may eventually tire of the inequities in the relationship.

> *Those who love money will never have enough. How absurd to think that wealth*

brings true happiness!
Ecclesiastes 5:10 NLT

When the wife bears the economic responsibility for the family, this violates God's original plan for the family. The husband was designed to be the provider for the family. This was never meant to be the role of the wife. If the wife is the chief financial resource for the household, this should be by choice not because of necessity.

It may be difficult if not impossible, for the wife to submit to her husband when it means relinquishing control of her resources to someone who has assumed the role of the receiver in the relationship. It can also be tempting for the wife who is the primary breadwinner to justify not submitting in a marriage.

***Be strong and steady, for you know that nothing you do for the Lord is ever useless.* 1 Corinthians 15:58 NLT**

If the receiver in the relationship is not in a relationship with God, the receiver may easily become the consumer in the relationship. They may assume they have the right to receive from the giver. It can also be difficult for the man to adjust to the wife being the primary breadwinner in the family. This can become emasculating.

In a relationship where the woman is the spiritual and economic head of the house, it leaves minimal opportunity for the husband to become the head of the house. A spouse cannot rule or lead in areas where they have no knowledge. As with any other occupation, this role requires preparation. God's grace is able to prepare us for any responsibility. Unless there is a shift in household responsibility, the person will remain the head of the house who bears the bulk of the weight for the household management and support.

> *And the LORD God said, It is not good that the man should be alone; I will make him an help meet for him.* **Genesis 2:18**

Each spouse should strengthen the other spouse. Where one spouse is weak, the other should be strong. The wife's duty and responsibility are to be a *help meet* for her husband. God provides through the wife the things that the husband needs to become successful. If the husband's pride hinders him from accepting the help that God has provided him through his wife, it hinders his potential for growth. Inadvertently, he sets himself up for failure. If the husband requests help and the wife does not freely provide it, she moves outside her God-given role. By destroying the order of the family, she sets the family up for failure.

> *We are pressed on every side by troubles, but we are not crushed and broken. We are perplexed, but we don't give up and quit.* **2 Corinthians 4:8 NLT**

A godly wife will find comfort in relinquishing her role when she is prepared to trust her husband to fulfill his role as the head of the family. When trust has been violated, it is not easily restored. When the injured spouse is able to show the offending spouse a measure of God's grace, trust can be restored. The person who wants to be trusted must maintain a standard of trustworthiness. If the person continues to practice tricks of deceit, it will further impede the process of restoring trust to the relationship. If deceitful practices are foregoing for an extended period, it will be impossible to restore trust without the grace of God.

Give thanks to the LORD and proclaim His greatness. Let the whole world know what He has done. **Psalm 105:1 NLT**

Without total submission to God, trust, honesty, thanksgiving, and grace, marriage is in danger of ending in betrayal or divorce. In any marriage, God's grace is able to sustain the marriage. When the spouses do not totally submit to God, order is not established in the household. It is only grace that holds any marriage relationship together.

Those who live only to satisfy their own sinful desires will harvest the consequences of decay and death. But those who live to please the Spirit will harvest everlasting life from the Spirit. **Galatians 6:8 NLT**

The reasons for choosing to stay married can be just as varied as the reasons for choosing divorce. The spouses may choose to remain married because of spiritual, social, financial, contractual, economic, or family commitments. These marriages are for convenience sake only. What happens when the convenience is no longer convenient?

All of you should be of one mind, full of sympathy toward each other, loving one another with tender hearts and humble minds. **1 Peter 3:8**

The marriage of convenience may become inconvenient. In relationships where the spouses choose to remain married for the sake of the children, the children often become the victims. In these cases, it places an unfair burden on the children. They may gain an unhealthy concept of marriage.

There are no easy solutions. When marriage ends in divorce, the children may also assume responsibility for its failure. When a marriage of convenience becomes inconvenient, everyone suffers.

Epilogue

For they being ignorant of God's righteousness, and going about to establish their own righteousness, have not submitted themselves unto the righteousness of God.
Romans 10:3

And the story ends. I would love to conclude this book with a fairy tale ending. However, in real life, there is no prince charming on a white horse who is able to sweep you off your feet. There is no 'happily ever after.' Marriage is a commitment before God and man. It is a legal and religious vow to join together to become one flesh. Its express purpose is that a man and woman join together forsaking all others until the conclusion of their earthly lives.

Today, there are many reasons why marriage ends. It is not my intention to preach for or against divorce. I'm not offering a moral judgment concerning divorce. Divorce has its function in society. It is my desire that marriage not be entered into lightly. It should not be considered as a transient state. Marriage is a commitment to pray and love even when the love is not convenient and when all hope appears to be gone. A ceremony and legal forms provide the legal commitment, but only God can unite two people into one. In marriage, both individuals must keep their individuality within their union. Each partner's strengths and weaknesses enter into this union.

"Suppose a woman is married and living in her husband's home when she makes a vow

or pledge. If her husband hears of it and does nothing to stop her, her vow or pledge will stand. But if her husband refuses to accept it on the day he hears of it, her vow or pledge will be nullified, and the LORD will forgive her. So her husband may either confirm or nullify any vows or pledges she makes to deny herself. But if he says nothing on the day he hears of it, then he is agreeing to it. If he waits more than a day and then tries to nullify a vow or pledge, he will suffer the consequences of her guilt."
Numbers 30:10-15 NLT

It is better not to make a vow than to make one and break it. Entering into my third marriage with my husband, I decided that this time I would work with him to fight to preserve our union and keep our family together. My daughter, Earline considers this to be our fourth marriage because we once renewed our vows. Four times, we have promised before God, our family, and civil authorities that we would bear each other's infirmities, share our highs as well as our lows, and strengthen each other. Each time, it was our intention that our marriage would flourish and edify ourselves and the family that we created. The honeymoon period would always be romantic and idyllic. Rather than focusing on working out the core issues in our marriage, we were swept up into a new romantic and exciting relationship. Viewing the relationship through rose-colored glasses, we dreamed of the perfect union.

Ye shall not need to fight in this battle: set yourselves, stand ye still, and see the salvation of the Lord with you, O Judah and Jerusalem: fear not, nor be dismayed; tomorrow go out against them: for the Lord will be with you. **2 Chronicles 20:17**

Now that we have matured, we are aware that no relationship is perfect. We are keenly aware of each other's flaws and strengths. Years of turmoil and strife enable us to see clearly each other's weaknesses and the ability to amplify them. It is easy to denigrate and destroy each other and our marriage. It takes the Lord to overcome years of emotional abuse on both sides. It takes time and patience to locate and edify the strengths in our relationship. We must constantly ask Him to guide us and order our steps in His Word.

Give your burdens to the LORD, and He will take care of you. He will not permit the godly to slip and fall. **Psalm 55:22 NLT**

During the difficult times, it is convenient to think of divorce. For us, divorce is a temporary solution to our communication problems. While arguing, it often feels that all love and hope is gone. These are the times that God's grace is sufficient to sustain the marriage. While tempers are flaring, it seems as if life apart is the desired state.

Thou wilt shew me the path of life: in Thy presence is fulness of joy; at Thy right hand there are pleasures for evermore.
Psalm 16:11

Following each divorce, the separation allowed us to reevaluate the importance of our marriage and our spouse's significance in our lives. Each time we divorced, the marriage was dissolved legally, but not emotionally. The connection between us is always clearer when we are separated. Money is needed to purchase a house, but God is needed to make a home. In order to sustain our marriage, we must pray without ceasing. The Lord is able to keep that which is committed unto Him. Often, we attempt to salvage a marriage, but without God, it is pointless. Except the Lord keeps the city, the watchman laboreth in vain.

And thus it is...***His grace is still sufficient for me...Even when it seems my faith is under FIRE!!!***

Other Titles
By
Dr. Charlotte Russell Johnson

ISBN 0974189308 *ISBN 0974189316* *ISBN 0974189324*

ISBN 0974189332 *ISBN 0974179340* *ISBN 0974189359*

ISBN 0974189369 *ISBN 0974189375* *ISBN 0974189383*

Reaching Beyond, Inc.
www.charlotterjohnson.com

Helping hurting humanity to reach beyond the barriers in their life, one barrier at a time.

ORDER FORM

Know someone else in crisis, or in need of encouragement order additional copies of this book to sow seeds of healing grace.

Postal Orders:

Reaching Beyond, Inc.
P. O. Box 12364
Columbus, GA 31917-2364
(706) 573-5942
Email us at: admin@charlotterjohnson.com
Please send the following book(s).

Qty.	Title	
____	*A Journey to Hell and Back*	$14.95 each
____	*The Flip Side*	$15.95 each
____	*Daddy's Hugs*	$12.95 each
____	*Grace Under Fire*	$14.95 each
____	*Mama May I*	$14.95 each
____	*Mama's Pearls*	$14.95 each
____	*Breaking the Curse*	$14.95 each
____	*Kissin' Hell Goodbye*	$14.95 each
____	*Oil for the Wounded*	$14.95 each

Sales tax:
Please add 7% for books shipped to GA addresses.
Shipment:
Book rate $3.50 for the first book and $1.75 for each additional book.